Dogmatic Truths: What Dogs Teach Us About Life

SPENCER BOUDREAU, PHD

ISBN 978-1-7774545-0-0

Editor: Maya Khamala

Design and layout: Ted Sancton/Studio Melrose

This book is available for purchase on
the CanamBooks Store: www.canambooks.com/store

This book was set in Scala Pro 13/21

THIS BOOK IS DEDICATED
to all the dogs in my life,
with gratitude for all they have taught me.

ACKNOWLEDGEMENTS

ANY SUCCESS I HAVE EVER had is due in large part to my wonderful wife, Susan, who is always there to inspire me to become a better version of myself. I can't count how many times she encouraged me to get back to my book and provided the support I needed to stay confident and accomplish my task. Merci ma Belle.

I would be remiss if I did not thank my daughter Brigitte who spent hours going over my manuscript and giving me valuable feedback. I am fortunate to have an English professor in the family.

Finally, I want to thank my many friends and acquaintances who shared their dog stories. You all helped demonstrate the many ways in which dogs are such valuable and enriching companions.

CONTENTS

INTRODUCTION

IN 2002, I HAD THE PRIVILEGE of visiting Pompeii with my daughter Brigitte. Being an avid student of ancient Rome, I marveled at the ruins of Roman life frozen in time over 2000 years ago by volcanic ash. At one point during my visit, I came across a beautiful mosaic of a dog with the inscription *Cave Canem* (Beware of the Dog). This was my first visit to Pompeii, but I had seen this artwork before in my high school Latin textbook. Needless to say I was thrilled and could not resist buying a copy of this mosaic in the souvenir shop.

The ancient Romans loved their dogs, and there are tender obituary messages to them on tombstones in cemeteries where they are buried alongside their masters. The human-dog relationship, however, goes back much further. Animal behaviorist John Bradshaw says there is evidence that this unique rapport began over 30,000 years ago: "We kept dogs before we invented writing, before we had permanent homes, before we grew crops."[1] Other scholars, like Yuval N. Harari, describe this special relationship as well: "The dog was the first animal domesticated by *Homo Sapiens,* and this occurred *before* the Agricultural Revolution."[2] These were working dogs who alerted humans to danger and accompanied them while hunting.

A number of scholars, like Hungarian ethologist Adam Miklosi, have published research regarding the uniqueness and origins of the dog-human relationship. Miklosi notes that "... the special role that dogs have played within human society is longstanding, and early humans shared an intimate bond or mystical/sacral relationship with their four-legged companions."[3] This is certainly easy to believe since it is common for a dog owner to refer to Fido as "a member of the family," and the loss of a dog is one of the most traumatic experiences a family can endure.

Our love affair with dogs continues to this day. There is

no community on earth where dogs are absent. However, if one has seen any of the SPCA fundraiser adds, it is clear that too many dogs are kept in disgraceful situations and need to be rescued. In addition, feral dogs are a serious problem in many communities – a situation I witnessed in India. However, surveys show that a total of about 78 million dogs live in households in the United States as pets[4] and billions of dollars are spent annually on our animal companions.[5] With the number of dog owners and the expenses involved in their upkeep, it is no wonder that many doggy-related businesses are booming.

In this book I wish to explore humanity's love affair with these canine creatures, while at the same time remembering the dogs in my own life. Friends and acquaintances, with little prompting, have also shared experiences which show how they were enriched by their dogs' presence. I also want to iterate the virtues that dogs display and what we can learn from them that will enhance our lives and make us better people. I sense that if you came upon this book, it may not be too difficult to convince you of the overall positive role dogs play in our lives.

Part I

My Dogs

*Dear God, please help me be
the person my dog thinks I am.*

PRAYER SEEN ON A BUMPER STICKER

My dad with his dog Major (probably from the 1930s) on the bay near my home fishing smelts. I remember my father telling me how much Major loved to eat fresh, raw smelts.

CURLY

As far as I know, my dad never had a dog growing up. I suppose my grandparents were too busy raising nine children, and the additional expense and responsibility of training and raising a puppy would have been too much for a family with an income that could barely cover essentials like food and shelter. However, my dad always loved dogs. He was never a cat person. He told me about the dogs he had after he was married, and I have pictures of him proudly posing with one of his favourites.

There is some convincing research that indicates growing up with pets leads to pet ownership in later life: "The evidence points to a robust link between the experience of living with pets during childhood and a person's attitudes, later in life, to animals in general, including but not limited to pets."[6]

I believe that my dad's love of dogs did rub off on me and my brother. But I had a love for animals in general. As a little boy, I even started a "Be Kind to Animals Club." I had learned that if we suffer here on earth (Catholicism referred to earth as a "valley of tears"), we could still hope for the joy of heaven, but animals, it was believed, did not have eternal souls, so my reasoning was that we had to help them have a good life here on Earth. I'm not so sure any more about the belief that animals don't go to heaven, but I still believe it is important to be kind to animals. All the animals I had growing up – rabbits, chickens, hamsters, pigeons – and all those that I took care of at summer camp – horses, ponies, and a fox named Freddy – taught me something. But of all God's creatures, my dogs were my wisest teachers – and the most lovable ones, too.

My first dog was named Curly. He was a cocker spaniel and he was my constant companion growing up. According to the American Kennel Club there are 13 official colours for cocker spaniels and Curly was more on the golden end of the spectrum. I recall him arriving at the train station as an adorable puppy in a little wooden box. In his later years, Curly got a bit chubby but he was always ready to follow me wherever I went around my hometown of Dalhousie, which is located on a bay in the northeastern region of New Brunswick, Canada – a great place to be a dog owner. Curly would follow me everywhere – to the beach, to the store, around the town, and all the while he was never tied up or on a leash. If I was going downtown (mere minutes from my home) and did not want him to follow me, I would say: "Curly, go home," and he would immediately turn back and go home with his head down and his tail between his legs. Normally, he slept in the basement, but I remember one time when my parents were away, I stayed with a family friend, Mrs. Chaisson. She let Curly sleep in the bedroom with me and I was thrilled. He would start out on the bed but when I woke up in the morning, he had always moved to a cooler spot on the floor. When observing a child interacting with his or her dog, it's obvious that one is beholding a mutually loving relationship. Author Jeffrey Moussaieff Masson writes, "Love for a dog during childhood is one of the deepest and purest emotions we are ever likely to have, and it remains with us for the rest of our lives."[7] I could not agree more.

When I was 13, Curly was old in dog years, but would still follow me everywhere. One day, our neighbour Mrs. Cool asked me to go to the store for her. There were two small stores very near my home, Jackson's, a convenience store, and Butland's just across the street. Butland's was a butcher shop and the owner often gave me a bone for Curly. I was going to Jackson's that day, and Curly noticed me going up the hill and ran after me, thinking I was going to Butland's. He waited there, but when he saw me returning home on the opposite side of the street he ran to catch up and was hit by a truck. I remember Curly's piercing cry of agony, and I ran to his side as fast as I could. There he was, lying on the side of the road with his little body half crushed. Even then, in agony and dying, he tried to wag his tail when he saw me. I ran home to tell my father and he called the police. I was in my room in tears when I heard a loud bang and I asked my dad, "Was that a car backfiring?" It was wishful thinking on my part. An RCMP police officer had put Curly out of his misery, but it didn't have the same effect on me.

The passing of a pet is frequently the first experience of mortality for children. It was not for me, since my mother had died suddenly two years previous, two days after her 46th birthday. I had just turned eleven years old. My only real consolation at that time was my faith and the belief that my mother, a kindhearted devout woman, was in heaven. Curly was my loyal companion during this sad period in my life. He could sense my deep sorrow as he accompanied me on our long walks along the seashore. The Franciscan priest Father Richard Rohr has written that the experiences of love and suffering have the potential to open us up to a mature vision of ourselves and of others. Suffering however, which he describes as the experience of not being in control, is a really tough life-teacher. Curly helped me through a very difficult time following my mother's death and taught me what it means to be faithful to the very end. His death made me realize that I really did love him, and regretfully probably took him for granted most of the time.

Curly and I when I was 10

It is evident to me that my love for God's creatures as a child was ethically founded in my Catholic Faith. Pope John Paul II proclaimed that animals are the "fruit of the creative action of the Holy Spirit and merit respect," and are "as near to God as men are." Pope Paul VI (not Pope Francis as originally reported) is said to have stated that, "One day, we will see our animals again in the eternity of Christ. Paradise is open to all of God's creatures."[8] If he is right, I think Curly made it to heaven. I hope I do too, by putting into practice what that cocker spaniel taught me: be kind and loving to others, even when it hurts to do so, and never take life or love for granted.

Pope Francis with a rescue dog

All his life he tried to be a good person.
Many times, however, he failed.
For after all, he was only human.
He wasn't a dog.

CHARLES M. SCHULZ

MAO

AT THE AGE OF 14, I left home to finish high school in a junior seminary in Massachusetts. It was a journey that lasted 14 years, as I had entered a Roman Catholic religious congregation known as the Salesians of Don Bosco. We gave up a lot in the seminary, and we were told we should not be attached to anything or anyone – even friends, let alone pets. It was the same situation for other religious orders. Even Franciscans, whose founder St. Francis had a particularly strong love for all of God's creatures, were not allowed to have pets. As noted by Franciscan Father Rich Rohr, "In most communities dogs or cats were forbidden."

My dogless situation persisted for about 10 years through novitiate, college, and a couple of years of teaching. After I graduated from college, I was assigned to teach at a school in Sherbrooke, Quebec. The Salesians also had a summer camp for boys who came from low-income families. The camp was set on a beautiful lake in a rural area a few miles from the school. At one point, I convinced my superiors that the boys would enjoy having a dog at the camp, and I was given permission to adopt a puppy from the SPCA. I named him Mao. He fit in perfectly, and he had the run of the camp. At the end of the camp season, my superiors thought I would bring him back to the SPCA. Instead, Mao ended up back at the school with me. He was great company, but it wasn't always easy to take care of him – especially since having a dog in the community was frowned upon by the powers that be.

There were adventures with Mao that I will never forget. He liked to roam the neigbourhood looking for a mate, for he had not been neutered (mea culpa). One time I went looking for him with a Salesian confrere. We finally located him. Locked in copulatory throes, Mao was experiencing a joyride down a hill linked butt-to-butt with his "Belle de Jour." I had never seen such a sight in my life. I later understood that this "butt to butt" position was very normal for dogs during copulation and is called the mating tie. Due to the situation, we were too embarrassed to stop the car to pick him up, so we drove around the block and came back to where we had seen him. By that time he had been "released" and was sitting on the side of the road, exhausted. We yelled "Viens, Mao," (he only understood French), and hoped no one would see him get in our car. Unfortunately, the owner of the female dog found out because he called our school some time later and asked us if we had a black and white dog. I sheepishly replied that we did. Thankfully he was not angry (his son went to our school). Later he told us his dog had a litter of puppies and there were a number which were black and white – future members of the clergy, he joked. I asked if I could go see the pups and he welcomed me – with Mao, who did not seem to have any paternal interest in his offspring. He rather looked in denial, but you didn't need a DNA test to identify the father of those adorable scamps. I was not aware of Mao having any other conquests, but I do know that he liked to check out the neighbourhood every once in a while. One time, he got his leg caught in a trap and needed to get a cast. One of the priests kindly paid for the vet bill. The cast didn't slow Mao down. I would see him running across the field with his front right leg in a cast straight out in front of him. It was quite a sight!

One day, I was duped by one of the students who called

me up posing as a parent while recording our telephone conversation. There was a popular French radio show at the time where people were phoned and duped about some completely fabricated issue. The student did not plan to put the recording on the radio, but it did make the rounds of the school. The call came after I had coached a hockey game and was upset by the loss. I took the call and the person on the other end asked me if I had a dog at the school. I said yes, and then he said his son went to the school and that my dog had urinated on his pant leg. I was stunned, then annoyed. It was Saturday, so I asked him what his son was doing at the school on a Saturday. He replied that it didn't matter and that a school wasn't a place for dogs. Now I was really getting angry and replied that I lived at the school, it was my home, and I could have any pets I wanted. He continued to show aggression and asked who was going to pay for the cleaning of his son's stained pants. I replied that I thought his son had peed his pants and blamed it on my dog. I finally got him to tell me who was calling, and gradually realized that he was a grade 11 student from our school who was very proud of his coup. The next day you can be sure the students teased me about the conversation. My younger confreres chuckled about the incident while some of the older ones looked at me with disapproval because of accusing the student of wetting his pants.

When I started my studies in theology at university, I would go out to the Salesian summer camp on weekends in the fall. I had the whole place to myself and was able to complete a lot of academic assignments. I would always bring Mao with me. He was great company and loved being there. At one point two other dogs showed up – one bigger than Mao, and one smaller. I didn't know their names but since I had a Mao (who was in power in China at that time), I baptized them Nixon and Pompidou – the American and French presidents of the day. They would play just like kids – hiding in the grass and jumping out at one another as they ran by. It didn't take long before Nixon and Pompidou were waiting for Mao whenever I arrived, and the fun would begin again. There was never any aggression among them.

After many years of religious life, I decided to leave the Salesian Congregation and set out on my own. I had a small basement apartment that I rented while I finished my second undergraduate degree, but I was not allowed a dog, so I had to leave Mao behind. It was difficult. The Salesians kept him for a while but then decided that he was too much to take care of and he was brought back to the SPCA. I don't know if he was adopted again but I do hope he was. I can honestly say that he enriched my life throughout a difficult

period when I was pondering whether to leave the congregation or not. When I did, it was like a divorce for me after
almost 14 years of religious life. In the evenings during that
time I would sit with Mao in my room. He had become my
therapy dog. I also think that Mao had a great life while we
were together. I understand why we were told in religious
life that we should not be attached to anything because
when that attachment is severed you experience pain. Yet
I believe that my time with Mao gave me ample pleasure to
outweigh the pain I experienced when we parted.

Mao as a puppy at summer camp

My cat confession

I HAVE A CAT CONFESSION to make. As I said, I have always
loved God's creatures, but was never really a cat person –
with one exception. In my first apartment I was not allowed
a dog, but I was allowed a cat. I purchased a Siamese cat because I was told the breed was as close to a dog as you could
get in the feline world. Apparently the hearsay was true because later I read that, "The Siamese is an overly energetic,
affectionate animal. It tends to be very vocal and is considered highly intelligent. The Siamese is dog-like in nature
and is one of the few breeds that will walk on a leash with
an owner."9

Lotus was a beautiful creature and she had a lot of character and followed me around like a dog. Unfortunately,
again, I had to give her up since I was moving to Montreal
and could not bring her with me. My vet adopted her, and
I knew she would have a good home. I will always remember Lotus as my in-between-dog-fix, a special cat who
thought she was a dog.

The better I get to know men,
the more I find myself loving dogs.

GENERAL CHARLES DE GAULLE

TEDDY

I LEFT THE SALESIANS at 28 and lived in apartments until a year after I got married at 33. I did not have a dog during that time. Susan, my spouse, had a dog growing up but she was not originally a dog person like I was (she certainly has become one since). After a year living in an apartment, Susan and I bought a home on a large property in rural Quebec. Just before we moved in, my brother surprised us with a gorgeous Airedale puppy. My dad had located a breeder in Sussex, New Brunswick and my brother bought him for us. For the next 30 years we were Airedale people. Teddy, our first family dog, whose official name was Theodore Bear Boudreau, was the most beautiful of all the dogs we owned. My mother-in-law, Mary, gave him his name because she thought he looked just like a teddy bear.

Soon after Teddy arrived, we had our first baby, Brigitte.

Teddy was not used to a baby in the house and when Brigitte would wake up at night crying, Teddy would howl from another part of the house and this created a sort of stereo effect to say the least! Brigitte loved Teddy. Like all parents, we wondered what her first word would be – mama or dada? Well, it was neither. It was "Ted." We were proud parents, both of our beautiful little girl and our handsome pup. One summer day, we decided to show them both off on a stroll through Old Montreal to see who would get the most attention. There was no contest. All we heard was "Regarde le chien, regarde le beau chien" ("Look at the dog, look at the beautiful dog"). We were quite surprised that Teddy attracted more attention than our beautiful baby girl. On another occasion we went to a photographer's studio to have a family pictured taken. We wanted one with Brigitte and Teddy but had no intention of asking for a picture of Teddy alone. The photographer was so impressed by Teddy that he insisted on taking a picture of him alone at no extra cost. Teddy looked so regal in his photo that it subsequently became known as his graduation photo.

When Teddy was still a puppy, we went to New Brunswick to visit my family. We stayed at my brother's cottage and Teddy met my brother's golden retriever, Tess, who was much older and much more mature. Teddy was fascinated by Tess and never ceased vying for her attention. He would constantly try to play with her, and at one point Tess, normally a very patient dog, promptly sat on Teddy as a final attempt to keep him from bothering her. It seemed to work, as she was much heavier than him!

My brother's cottage was on the banks of the Restigouche River and the river was close enough to the Baie-des-Chaleurs to have tides. Teddy would go down the steep bank and wander way out when the tide was low. We could barely see him from the cottage. We would yell after him and he would come bounding back with low-tide mud all the way up his legs. It looked like he was wearing black nylons. Yet Teddy did not always come home when we called him. Whenever he had the chance to escape, he would. You could call his name for an hour but there would be no sign of him. Our home is surrounded by a wooded area and Teddy loved the woods – a natural habitat for an Airedale. Once, he was gone for two days and we thought that we would never see him again. On the second night, Susan and I were in bed and we heard something outside our bedroom window panting in the backyard. A very dirty Teddy had returned, covered in burrs and dirt that required a major cleaning before he could re-emerge!

We thought that obedience training would help, so for

several Saturdays we took Teddy to a respectable obedience school. We were impressed by the other dogs who seemed to be way ahead of Teddy when it came to learning commands. Some of the owners were very competitive and vying for first place for their dogs in the competition to be held at the end of the course. We had no such aspirations. We were correct not to because later on I learned that his somewhat erratic behavior was typical of his breed. As Dog expert Stanley Coren notes, "Terriers don't do well in obedience simply because they have been bred to be independent and loners."[10] After several weeks of training and many hours of practice, competition day arrived, and the dogs had several commands to follow. Teddy did more or less OK on some routine tasks, but the most important test was for the dogs to remain sitting while their owners left the room. Teddy stayed in place but sat a bit sideways on his hip with his leg sticking out from under him. This was not classic form. One of the dogs was in heat and the trainers told us that this would make the test even more challenging. We watched from a window and the owner of the German shepherd boasted that her dog would likely take first place since he had shown potential during the course. She was shocked when her dog, along with others, got up because of the female in heat. Teddy just sat there sloppily and did not move, probably more oblivious than obedient. When the judging was over, the trainers started with third place. Teddy didn't make third place so we dared to think that he might make second place. Then the trainers announced who had won second place – it was the German shepherd. It seemed Teddy had lost out on a prize, but as it turned out, we were wrong. Susan and I started to giggle because we couldn't believe that Teddy, our run-away Teddy, our strong-willed Teddy, had won first prize! As we walked up to claim it, Susan whispered to me, "This is embarrassing." On the drive home Teddy sat proudly between us with his large first place ribbon hanging from his collar. He seemed to be thinking, "I fooled all of you, didn't I?" He sure had, and we had a good laugh all the way home. His first-place ribbon was prominently displayed for years on our summer porch and when visitors saw it, they would remark with a quizzical, "Really?" One thing I learned about Airedales over the years is that they know when to make a run for it and they know when it's useless to try because there is no better option than doing nothing. I think that is what happened to Teddy that day. Why he wasn't interested in the female in heat – I really don't know.

Teddy was the only dog we owned that we ever considered breeding. We found out that there was an owner of a female Airedale not far from us, and he agreed to bring his dog over to spend the day cavorting with Teddy. We had hopes that he would become a daddy. At the end of that day I saw the most exhausted dog I have ever seen in my life. He flopped down and would not or could not move. It wasn't for lack of effort, but let's just say that *it* didn't happen. I was then told that sometimes you have to "guide" the dog's member into the female for best results. That was the last of our attempts at breeding. Teddy could have used Mao for some proper "guidance," whose first attempt at mating resulted in pregnancy for his mate. But Mao wasn't available, and Teddy was not going to get any guidance from me.

Teddy would never miss an opportunity to run away when he could. On one occasion, he started out running up the street towards the woods and Susan noticed that he had suddenly stopped and could not run anymore. This was not the Turbo-Ted we knew. Something was wrong. We took him to the vet, who–showed us the X-ray that revealed several lesions on his lungs. Teddy had lung cancer. He was 10, and the vet said we could decide to put him down right away or later. We decided to wait, and he told us we would know when it was time. We were all obviously very upset and were certainly not ready to part with him yet. It was a quiet car ride back to the house. The vet was right. I did know when it was time for Teddy to be euthanized. He had stopped eating regular dog food, so I started cooking hamburger for him. He ate it for a while but at one point he stopped eating anything I would offer him. He was going to starve to death, so we made the decision to bring him to the vet one last time. This was not a quiet car ride. There was lots of sobbing, and Teddy seemed sweeter and more affectionate than ever. At the vet's we said one last goodbye. It was all over in seconds. We left, in tears again, with a clipping from his coat. I often notice that dog owners seem to be more upset about the loss of their dog than a good number of relatives, and having had Teddy in my life, I understand why. Teddy was our first family dog, and, despite his strength and stature, he was a gentle giant.

This photo of Brigitte and Teddy was displayed in the photographer's studio window for quite some time.

If you want a friend in Washington,
get a dog.

Harry S. Truman

Cayce

I'm sure many of you would agree it takes a while to get over the death of a cherished pet. It makes you wonder if you should really go through the whole experience again. I have the habit, however, of not being able to resist visiting the SPCA. On one visit to the Montreal SPCA shortly after the death of Teddy, I asked if anyone ever brought Airedales in for adoption and the response was that it happened – but rarely. I then asked if someone could call me if they did get one and they told me that it was against their policy to do so. I guess someone didn't mind bending the rules, since soon after my visit I got a call and was told that an Airedale had been dropped off. I also understood that if I did not come that very day he would not be around for long. Apparently he would be euthanized since he was 2 years old, and already considered an older dog. I think it was more the fact that he was an Airedale and the thinking was that not everyone can handle Airedales. When I got to the SPCA it was love at first lick. Now I only had to convince Susan. I called her and she came to see him with my two youngest children. We were all in a small square space so we could get acquainted in the hope that the relationship would work out. The children were taken aback by Cayce's uncontrollable enthusiasm for his new family. Susan`s first reaction was "Oh, he's cute," and I knew I had her. Our positive interaction with Cayce only confirmed our decision.

His previous owners had brought him to the SPCA because they said they were moving into an apartment and could not keep him. In his file it was noted that his previous name was Rambo. I knew that wouldn't work for Susan. It was also noted in French, "Not to be adopted as a first dog – consider the breed." As previous owners of an Airedale, it did not take any convincing for them to believe we could handle him. Of course, one can never be sure with an Airedale.

The children did not know what we were up to that day. When the school bus arrived and Brigitte saw Cayce on the lawn, her scream of delight could be heard throughout the neighbourhood. Cayce could not have received a warmer welcome. The name Cayce came from a popular children's

TV show in Canada called Mr. Dressup. Mr. Dressup's two puppets were called Finnegan and Casey. Finnegan was the dog's name, but we preferred Casey, so Rambo became Cayce – with a new spelling. Our new dog had gone from a cage at the SPCA to an acre in the country. He had won the lottery. He wasn't really a country dog and he had to get used to my chickens and rabbits. But he quickly adapted, and the children loved him. He was not the beauty Teddy was – and the children were convinced he had a peculiar body odor, but he was an Airedale, and he was ours.

Like Teddy, Cayce had a mind of his own when it came to obedience and he liked to take off when he could. It was somewhat amusing because he would be running down the street and I would be calling him, and sweet loveable Cayce would look back at me over his shoulder while running and bark at me. It was a very disobedient response, like when you tell a child it's time to leave the park and he shouts "No!" Once Cayce ran away to a neighbour's – just a few houses from us. I thought that I would never see him again because my neighbour had the biggest German shepherd I had ever seen – aptly named Magnum. He had come over to my place once, knocked over a rabbit hutch and killed one of my rabbits. I followed Cayce to Magnum's expecting to see a dead Airedale – or at least a badly injured one. Instead I witnessed two dogs having fun playing together. I guess you can't judge a dog by its size, but I assure you that I would never have attempted to play with Magnum.

Cayce was very gentle and loved to have his belly scratched while lying on his back – so much so that he would poke me with his paw if I stopped. However there was one incident that happened with him which was totally out of character. My son Justin came home from elementary school one day and jumped on Cayce's back. It may have been the simple fact that he was very startled, or he may even have had a bad hip. He had also just received an injection from the vet. Whatever the reason, instinctively he turned and bit Justin in the face. My wife and son were totally shocked, but I think Cayce was too. After some panic, and advice from the vet, we realized that his reaction was not out of the ordinary for a dog in such a situation. Alexandra Horowitz wrote that dogs "are wired to act before contemplating action."[11] Justin's bite wound was superficial and left no scar. Neither Cayce nor Justin held a grudge about the incident.

Dog owners have stories that reveal astounding behaviour which can't always be explained. One I remember about Cayce involved school buses. When my four children were in school, several school buses would go up and down our street one after another, sometimes a minute or less apart. As far as I was concerned, the buses all looked and sounded alike. Not for Cayce. He would be lying on the front lawn and he knew exactly what bus the kids were on even before it stopped. He would jump up and do the "so happy to see you" dog dance. It was truly amazing.

The tough thing about being a dog owner is that we most often outlive them. The average lifespan of Airedales is ten to twelve years and that was the average lifespan for our Airedales. Since Cayce was older when we got him, we had him for about nine years. As author Agnes Sligh Turnbull says, "Dogs' lives are too short. Their only fault really." As far as I'm concerned, that was Cayce's only fault.

After Cayce died, I found this poem and it reminded me of how fortunate we were to find each other.

> My Shelter Days are numbered ten.
> Ten more days until my end.
> My Shelter Days are numbered eight.
> Please adopt me. Change my fate.
> My Shelter Days are numbered six.
> Adopt a pet week, still no one's pick.
> My Shelter Days are numbered four.
> Four more days and then no more.
> My Shelter Days are numbered two.

Someone will take me, I just don't know who.

My Shelter Days are numbered none.

I know I'm finished, then you come.

My Shelter Days are over, done,

Because you, my master, took me home.

– Courtney Bailey (from *The Final Countdown*)

*Heaven goes by favor. If it went by merit,
you would stay out and your dog would go in.*

MARK TWAIN

MONTY

MONTY, YET ANOTHER AIREDALE, was our next dog. My
youngest son Justin, who was about to start high school,
had to choose between getting a television or a dog for his
birthday. I was happy he chose a dog. The Airedale breeders
we contacted lived in western Québec, about a two-hour
drive from our home. Airedales have big litters so there
were several pups to choose from, minus the girls who were
already gone. My choice was made when one of the pups
came over and pulled on my shoelace, untying it. He was
to join our family. It was meant to be, as they say.

Monty, whose official name was Montgomery Poindexter
Boudreau, was only six weeks old when we brought him
home. I mentioned to the breeders that in my experience
Airedales were stubborn – "têtu" in French. They looked at
me with some annoyance and replied, "they have character."

I agreed. Not only do they have character, but they *are* characters – and Monty was quite the character. He knew how to get into trouble and at times the things he did were so funny you just had to laugh. One day while Susan was vacuuming our downstairs den, she had the impression that someone was watching her. Sure enough, when she looked up there was Monty's head poking through the window screen, apparently very interested in whatever she was doing. I had to replace a number of screens before Monty finally got the hint that we did not find it funny anymore. On another occasion, Monty got his priorities all wrong. Where we live, it is somewhat rural, and we keep chickens for their eggs. Although we never ate the chickens, local hawks have, on the rare occasion, tried to have our chickens for lunch. One day I looked out of my kitchen window and there was a hawk on top of our old doghouse consuming a chicken with surgical acumen. Unfortunately it was too late for me to do anything to save it. Afterwards, Susan asked me where Monty had been when all this was going on. "Oh Monty," I said, "He was in the front yard barking at a neighbour going by in his motorized wheelchair." After that, I understood that the chickens were on their own when it came to predators.

Then there was the time Monty decided to be a thief. My

son Patrick is the one who reminded me of this story. I had hired some guys to do minor construction work on my property and at one point one of the men asked me if I could stop Monty from stealing their tools. No sooner would they put down a screwdriver or hammer than Monty would grab it and take off with his booty. I found it quite comical that he was outmaneuvering and frustrating these big guys.

Monty also had his favourites when it came to visitors. He was always happy to see Pierre, our milkman, and Pierre was always happy to see him. He even liked the mailman and, contrary to what many dogs would do, he would run up to him looking for a friendly pat. One night though, Monty was sprayed by a skunk (my dogs never seemed to figure out that a skunk was not a cat), and we had not had time to bathe him before the mailman arrived the next morning. Monty greeted him as usual and even rubbed up against his pants. Needless to say, our mailman tried everything to clean the skunk smell out of his pants but finally gave up and got rid of them. He still liked Monty, but we had to reassure him that we would not let that sort of incident happen again.

A few weeks after Monty came to his new home, his breeders sent us a note reminding us to be firm when raising him, but also to be tender and loving. It reminded me of the "love and limits" advice for raising children. It makes sense, since the family dog more often than not *does* become a member of the family. Monty was indeed a member of our family and we christened him with several loving nicknames. Among these were MoMo, and The Little Man. He was great with the children and they really loved him. My daughter Brigitte wanted Monty to be part of her wedding party. She even asked Father Richard, the priest and family friend who performed the ceremony, if Monty would be allowed to come to the church for the wedding. He did not agree but Brigitte insisted that Monty be in the wedding pictures and with a few bribes he behaved very well during the photo sequence.

It was poor Brigitte who had to deal with Monty's unexpected death. It was Susan's birthday and we decided to go kayaking on the Chambly Basin near my home. That morning I noticed that Monty whimpered as he got up. I did not make much of it since he was 10 years old and Airedales tend to have some hip problems as they age. When we left home he was lying outside in the shade and seemed a bit lethargic. I did not bring my cell phone with me when I went kayaking so it would not get wet. When we returned to shore after a couple of hours, I noticed that there were several calls from home. I called home immediately and

Brigitte informed me that Monty had died. He had acted very strangely after we left, and she noticed him doing things he never did before. He seemed to be looking for a place to die and made an attempt to leave the property. Finally he went downstairs to the den, turned his back to Brigitte and collapsed facing a corner of the room. Needless to say we were shocked. The only medical explanation we got from the vet was that he likely died from bloat-gastric dilatation and volvulus. Unless someone is fully aware of this condition very early on and the dog has an operation, there is nothing to be done. Monty's strange behaviour before he died made me think that he just wanted to be by himself, find a quiet place, not bother anyone, and pass on. In her book *Inside of a Dog,* Alexandra Horowitz writes, "They are aware when they are damaged. Hurt or dying, dogs often make great efforts to move away from their families, canine or human, to settle down and perhaps die someplace safe."[12] Another referred to how an animal surrenders to death despite a will to live. "Even in dying they are teaching us. For the animal, death is easier. The animal can surrender into it, although, yes, there is a will to live."[13] It was a sad day for us as we wrapped his body in a blanket, put it in the car, and brought him to the vet's for cremation. Just recalling that time has provoked an emotional response from me. Monty was such a great dog and he brought us so much joy. This is the email my wife Susan wrote to the family after Monty died:

I feel like I have been in a slump since hearing the terrible news on Saturday about our Little Man.

How do you get over this? It takes time and you are going to feel sad. It's good to feel sad. Monty touched us all in a very special way. His love and appreciation for each and every one of us was unconditional.

I ask myself "What would Monty want?" Given a choice between sitting on the couch and reading or getting up and going for a walk-he would always choose the latter. So here's what I'm trying to do. I'm trying to move. I'm trying to set small goals and complete them. I'm thinking of Monty as I do them. I know he liked to be on the move.

So MoMo has become my inspiration. To move, to carry on. That's how I'm dealing with his passing right now.

Monty on the day of my daughter Brigitte's wedding
(Sept. 3rd, 2010)

What we have once enjoyed we can never lose.
All that we love deeply, becomes a part of us.

HELEN KELLER

Dogs love their friends and bite their enemies, quite unlike people, who are incapable of pure love and always have to mix love and hate.

SIGMUND FREUD

CHARLOTTE

MY MOST DIFFICULT EXPERIENCE with a dog was the one I had with Charlotte. After we lost Monty, we waited a while before considering another dog. There was an animal refuge not far from our home and we found out that they had a year-old Airedale for adoption. We visited the refuge and took Charlotte for a walk. She was perfect with us and since we had had a good experience with Cayce who was also a rescue dog, we were compelled to adopt her. Charlotte, we were told, was the product of a puppy mill. This was not a good beginning for her, and it has been observed that some dogs from puppy mills tend to be aggressive. Also, she was bought by a young family and was left in a cage all day when the owners were working. This wasn't good for her either, since Airedales are very high energy dogs. Apparently the last straw with Charlotte's owners occurred when a relative visited with her dog and Charlotte decided to take him on. We were told that the gentleman who brought her to the shelter was in tears when he left. I could totally relate to his experience later on.

Despite all these negatives, Charlotte was gentle with Susan and me. We decided to adopt her and since she needed a good bath, we stopped at a pet shop on the way home and asked if someone was available to bathe her. The owner was very kind and said that no one was available but that we could use the facility and bathe her ourselves. We gave her a thorough washing and brushing. She was perfect and she let us do what we had to do. The problem was, she didn't seem to like or trust anyone else. Dog researcher Miklosi points out, "With regard to aggression, the human–dog relationship is based on 'unconditional trust' (just like the human–human relationship). However, if this trust is lost for any reason, the original relationship will be difficult to reinstate."[14] During a family party soon after we had adopted her, we noticed that when some of our younger relatives went near her, she growled. We were somewhat alarmed since she had been so good with us. We decided to hire a dog trainer, Anne-Marie, who came to the house once a week and made some progress with Charlotte. At one point she brought her own dog, Zeus, a beautiful standard poodle, and Charlotte learned to play with him, somewhat roughly, but not aggressively. Charlotte also accepted the trainer and did not demonstrate any aggressiveness towards her. However Charlotte seemed to still only like Susan and me. She nipped at a friend and bit the leg of a close family friend who made a sudden move when next to her. We were getting tired of making excuses for her. Another incident that deeply concerned me occurred while I was jogging with Charlotte. Two little boys were playing in their front yard, and as we ran past them Charlotte growled. I thought to myself that I could never trust her with children.

The summer after we adopted her, we planned a trip to Europe and needed somewhere to board Charlotte. Our trainer recommended a place that boarded dogs. We visited a highly recommended kennel with Charlotte and the owner made it clear that she would have to get along with the other dogs since they were kept in a common enclosure. He then decided to test Charlotte to see how she would react with the other dogs. It was a disaster. Given an extra minute or two I think Charlotte would have killed the owner's little dog. I knew then that we could no longer keep her. We could not leave her with anyone, and we could not board her. When we got home, Susan contacted the shelter and told the owner that unfortunately it was not working out with Charlotte. She told us that we could bring her back and that the shelter had a no-kill policy. We had seen dogs referred to as "lifers" at the shelter because they could not be put up for adoption. Susan agreed that she had to be brought back but was too upset to go with me. Thankfully, my daughter Brigitte came (another person Charlotte actually seemed to like), because the 30-minute drive to the shelter seemed an eternity. We brought her in, and they put her in a pen next to "one of her former friends." The hardest part for me was when we were leaving. I could hear Charlotte barking and I knew exactly what she was saying – "Where are you going? You forgot me." I will never forget how deeply sorry I was for having to bring her back to the shelter. Like humans, dogs fear being abandoned. Charlotte's anxiety was real. When reviewing the dogs available at the SPCA in Montreal, the vast majority were described as having "separation anxiety." There are a number of reasons for returning a dog to a shelter, but studies show that the number one reason is aggression. The tendency to run away and hyperactivity appear to be the other most common reasons.[15] I had a lot of experience with hyperactive and disobedient Airedales, but not aggressive ones.

Interestingly, Gladys Brown Edwards in *The New Complete Airedale Terrier* notes that originally Airedales were bred to be aggressive to all but their master:

> Among the mine-pits of the Aire, the various groups of miners each sought to develop a dog which could outfight and outhunt and outthink the other mine's dogs. Bit by bit, thus, an active, strong, heroic, compactly graceful and clever dog was evolved – the earliest true form of the Airedale. Then the outer world's dog fancy got hold of him and shaped and improved him into the show-type Airedale of today...He is swift, formidable, graceful, big of brain, and ideal chum and guard...To his master he is an adoring pal. To marauders he is a destructive lightning bolt.[16]

I do not wish to get into the debate about whether there are bad dogs or just bad dog owners – or both. There is wide disagreement about this, and several jurisdictions have – to much protest – banned or greatly restricted particular breeds of dogs. One of the banned or maligned breeds in some jurisdictions is the pit bull. I found it interesting to discover a book with vintage portraits of children and their dogs, portraits taken mostly at the end of the 19th and beginning of the 20th centuries – in particular there was a portrait of an infant with a pit bull. The portrait, taken in 1910, has the following caption:

> At the turn of the twentieth century, pit bull-type dogs were immensely popular companion dogs and never considered untrustworthy around small children. In fact, the breed standard for American pit bulls, written in 1898, observes that these dogs "have always been noted for their love of children."[17]

Despite this, Professors Coppinger and Feinstein in their book, *How Dogs Work*, are blunt in their assessment that, "there are countless problematic dogs that are anything but good friends to humans."[18] They refer to the problem of feral dogs in poorer nations and the spread of rabies – and the millions of dog bites every year in the United States. Without overly anthropomorphizing (which the authors say is at the origin of the "man's best friend" belief), let's not forget that there will never be any creatures as violent and vicious as humans are to one another and to all of God's creations. I cannot but suspect that Charlotte's behaviour was linked to her experiences of neglect (the puppy mill) and isolation (she was in a cage for most of the day, for the first year of her life). It is easy to agree with Jeffrey Moussaieff Mason when he writes: "Any dog taken from a pound – or really, anywhere at all – has led a life with consequences that you may never come to know."[19] It is well established that early experiences for humans and animals alike establish the patterns that shape our ability to trust others (or not). All the dogs I had that came from positive environments turned out to be lovable, gentle companions. Susan has told me more than once that she loved Charlotte in a very special way and will never forget her as a wounded companion.

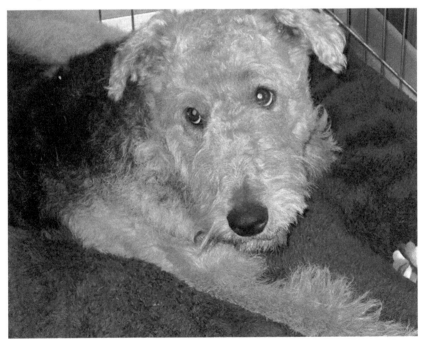

Charlotte

AIREDALES POST-SCRIPTUM

I WAS REMINDED RECENTLY of how our decades-long allegiance to Airedales began. When I was in college my younger brother and sister were in their teens and they managed to convince my father to get a dog. But my father was not going to make it easy for them. He agreed, but only on the condition that they save $100 in pennies – not just any pennies, but 1967 pennies – because it was Canada's centennial year. That's 10,000 pennies in one-dollar rolls for a total of 100 rolls. Long story short – they did it, and finally decided on an Airedale they named Cookie. Where there's a will, there's a way, and in this case, a wag.

*Whoever said you can't buy happiness
forgot little puppies.*

GENE HILL

MOLLY

AFTER OUR UNFORTUNATE EXPERIENCE with Charlotte, we hesitated for several months before getting another dog. Susan especially was very distraught by the experience. She had bonded strongly with Charlotte and because Charlotte behaved so with her, she had a difficult time acknowledging any of Charlotte's shortcomings. Also, we were not getting any younger and we planned to travel more in the future. Finally, grandchildren were on the horizon and we wanted to make sure that we could trust the new dog with the little ones.

Our daughter Vanessa finally convinced us to get another dog and try a new breed. I'll let her tell the story:

> When I returned home in the summer of 2012
> to complete my master's degree, I felt as though
> something was missing from my childhood home.

For the first time in my 27 years, I was without a dog. I recall late night talks with my parents, often over a few glasses of wine, where we would imagine our home with a dog. Shortly before, my parents had adopted an older dog, but were forced to bring her back due to her unpredictable nature. This particularly affected my mother, as she had grown attached to Charlotte and felt a deep void after we returned her. I remember my mother telling me that she was not sure if she was ready to love another dog.

One day, my father turned to my mother and said, "Will having a dog enrich our lives?" Without hesitation, my mother replied with an obvious "Well, yes." My father, who had grown up always having a dog, smiled and winked at me. I knew there was no turning back. We were getting a dog. Molly arrived that summer from Alberta. A Labradoodle puppy full of love, with an exorbitant amount of energy. Knowing her for the last 8 years, I have seen her mature into a beautiful companion – she has brought me so much joy. She's the kind of dog who gets you. The kind of dog who will see you cry and know exactly why. Molly got me through some of the most difficult times in my life, by simply being there. Her presence was my therapy. Molly is more of a people-dog; she doesn't care much for other dogs. Perhaps that's why I didn't find her in a room filled with other dogs, and why I was never faced with the choice of choosing her over another. Because let's face it, she chose me.

After a good amount of web surfing and some inquiries we settled on a Labradoodle – as Vanessa described – also known as a Labrador-Poodle mix. On the breeder's website Labradoodles were described as "people friendly." The breeders lived in Alberta and our little six-week old puppy had a long journey ahead of her. She was flown from Alberta with a stop-over in Toronto where she was put on a flight to Montreal. When we got notification that she had arrived we quickly went to the airport but were told we were at the wrong address and that we had to go further, to a cargo reception area. Finally at cargo, we found ourselves rushing around confusing corridors. Eventually, we found her in her little transport cage and blanket. The workers said that it was a good thing we finally got there because they were ready to keep her. The first thing we did was bring her outside so she could peè. I was amazed that despite a trip of thousands of miles plus a stopover in Toronto – a journey of more than twelve hours – she had not peed in her cage! We were immediately smitten. We named her Molly.

Molly as a puppy

Labrador retrievers and poodles are both considered intelligent breeds. I remember a friend saying that Airedales were not too bright. I took it personally and expressed my disagreement. Opinions aside, we instantly noticed that Molly was one smart pooch. She was housebroken almost immediately and early on she learned a few simple commands. Of course, we all had to get used to one another. I remember her first night in her travel cage. We put a clock in the cage with her to simulate her mother's heartbeat (we were told this was the effect). She was only six weeks old, after all. Well, either the old clock trick doesn't work, or it didn't work for Molly, because she cried for a good part of the night. At one point we wondered what we had gotten ourselves into. Susan, bleary eyed, remarked, "It's like having a new baby and I'm getting too old for this!" Luckily, Molly soon got over her night crying (a lot quicker than my four children did) and she adopted us as readily as we adopted her. One of the things that struck me about Molly as a puppy was that when she would run to me in the yard, she seemed to always have a smile on her face. I guess she still does, because on our walks with Molly in Florida during our vacation time there, one gentleman always referred to her as "Smiley."

Molly was certainly people-friendly and adapted very well to our pack, grandchildren included. It has become extremely evident to us that she prefers people to dogs, and she has even shown minor aggression to dogs much bigger than her. She is curious about cats but ironically immediately backs off when a cat lets her know that she is too close. Like most dogs, she likes to chase squirrels, and like most dogs, she never catches one. She also likes to run after my chickens but never catches them either, and I know she would never hurt them.

Molly certainly loves her creature comforts. She will stake out any couch, chair, pillow, or soft spot in a room as her own personal napping area. I know that this is not unusual for dogs, but Molly has perfected this art to an extent that I never observed with my other dogs. Our biggest concern about Molly is all the health ailments she has had – from hip dysplasia, to allergies, and regular ear infections. We have been to see more than one vet and even took her to the veterinary school of the Université de Montréal for an examination. She is on medication for the hip dysplasia and it has helped a lot, but we are still dealing with all her other conditions. We even did a blood test to find out what her allergies were. I was surprised to find out that she is allergic to beef. Despite all these ailments and the cost of dealing with them we are crazy about our little girl who is ready 24/7 to go for a car ride, show affection, or receive affection. If there is the slightest indication that I am going somewhere, especially when I pick up my car keys, she lets me know that she wants to accompany me, because she loves the car that much. So whether I am going to the grocery store, the gym, or just shopping in general, she loves to come along. Like all dogs, she loves the breeze and the smells she encounters as she sticks her head out the window. Also like all dogs, Molly likes to get her belly rubbed and knows how to communicate that. When I'm sitting in my La-Z-Boy, she will bang the side of the chair to let me know it's scratch-and-rub-the-belly-time. If I stop, she bangs again until I say no. She will eventually give up – until next time, or until she finds someone else to rub her. She's promiscuous that way.

After retirement, I decided I wanted to do some volunteer work at a hospital in Montreal. I went through the vetting process and during my tour of the hospital, we stopped at the psychiatric ward. The nurse who was giving the tour indicated that she would love to have a dog to do some pet therapy with the patients. After the tour I spoke to her privately and indicated that I had a little dog who was a possible candidate because she loved people, and in addition was hyper allergenic and did not shed. The nurse was interested and let me know that she would be in touch to arrange a trial visit to the ward. On the day of the visit, Molly calmly rode up in the elevator and was introduced to the staff and patients. At one point I asked the nurse how the test was going, and she looked at me said, "She aced it!" She then indicated that Molly would need an ID, so we went to the department where they make IDs and voila – Molly became the first canine volunteer in the hospital. I indicated to the nurse that I did not have my ID yet and she told me it wasn't ready yet but not to worry because as long as I was with Molly her ID would work for me too. Molly has been a huge hit at the hospital ever since. She gets an incredible welcome from the staff, who have to be reminded at times that she's there for the patients. I found it amusing that once when I was going up in the elevator, a nurse whom I did not know remarked, "Oh Molly, you got a haircut!" Often the nurses know Molly's name but are not quite sure about mine. Once, when I was leaving the hospital, a nurse shouted out, "Bye Molly," and to me – "You too."

The patients who so wish meet Molly in a common area and have a great time playing with her and giving her all the affection and attention she loves. They often tell me stories about the dogs they owned when they were younger or the dogs they now own. Research is clear about how therapeutic pet therapy can be for psychiatric patients. I recall one young woman saying, "I was hearing voices in my head until Molly got here, and now there are no more voices."

On one visit to the hospital, I was greeted outside the psychiatric ward by a doctor and two residents. The doctor asked if I would mind bringing Molly up to the geriatric floor to visit a lady who was 102, a widow with no children. The doctor told me that she had a particular love of dogs. Of course I agreed and the doctor entered her room and let her know that there was someone here to see her and that she would probably be pleased with the visit. The lady was indeed thrilled to see Molly. At one point she asked if I would put her on her bed. I glanced at the nurse who said, "Sure." Molly, always the comfort-lover, thoroughly enjoyed being on the bed and quickly made herself comfortable while being petted by this delightful lady. She said to me more than once that, "They know when you love them." The doctor told me that I made her day. On my next visit the doctor told me that Molly's visit was very therapeutic for his patient, and consequently she had improved considerably.

We hope Molly will be with us for several more years. She will probably be our last dog, but I can't say for sure.

Part II

WHAT MY FRIENDS SAY
ABOUT THEIR DOGS

*My father was a St. Bernard, my mother
was a collie, but I am a Presbyterian.*

MARK TWAIN (*A DOG'S TALE*)

FOR THE PURPOSES OF THIS BOOK, I also asked a number of my friends to write about how their dogs have enriched their lives. I was touched by their spontaneous and sincere texts. It is not unusual that we speak fondly of and remember our canine companions. We give our dogs biographies. We know them to be the subject of a life. To use the terms of the animal rights philosopher, Tom Regan, "They do not have stories to tell, but we have stories about them. We know of their infancies, sometimes their births, and their days of childhood, their glory days, and, with heartbreaking frequency, we recount their declines."[20]

Here, my friends tell their dog day stories:

ANNIE

AS BREEDERS OF GOLDEN RETRIEVERS, we sometimes have the opportunity to place a dog, once considered for breeding, which for one reason or another makes a better pet. Annie was just such a dog. She was a lovable girl who was a bit taller than the standard goldens, so we placed her.

Annie was perfectly suited to Pat, an older single woman in town who needed the company and had had dogs for many years. Besides, we would be close by, so we could assist if needed. It was a perfect fit that lasted quite a while until Pat became ill. We were called upon to take Annie home with us whenever Pat needed time in the hospital or went to see her doctor. However it became apparent after a time that Pat was very ill with stage four cancer, which was swiftly bringing things to an end.

One evening, we had a call from the hospital and the nurse said that Pat had asked to see Annie. She wasn't sure how it would work though, because Pat had since slipped into a coma. We decided to bring Annie anyway since we wanted to see Pat before she passed. Since Annie was not allowed in the hospital, my wife Laurie and I slipped up some back stairs with Annie and with the help of a few nurses, snuck her down the hall into Pat's room. I never expected what happened next. Annie rested her head on Pat's bed, close to her hand, and after a few minutes Pat began to stroke her head! She awoke, and in a soft voice began talking to Annie, not aware of our presence. After a few minutes, Pat slipped back into her coma and we left the room. None of us had expected Pat's reaction. We drove home with Annie, trying to figure out what had just happened. Walking into the house we heard the phone ringing. It was the hospital telling us that Pat had died just a few minutes after we left. The love we have for our pets is a powerful connection – so powerful that it can bring a dying woman out of a coma so she can say goodbye to her companion. Annie knew Pat wasn't well as she carefully laid her head on Pat's bed. It was love in action.

Jerry Stecker

Annie

ROSIE

I HAVE A FAMILY MEMBER that was adopted at twelve weeks old. Name: Rosalita, or Rosie for short. She came to us all the way from a farm in West Virginia. I had her tested to find out about her breed, because we knew her mother was a purebred golden retriever, but daddy was a rolling stone, so we didn't know the rest. Turns out he was 25% border collie and 25% boxer. I had had a golden before, so I knew she was fairly intelligent and with the border collie mix she took to training quickly. As things turned out, I got her right before I was diagnosed with cancer and she followed me around everywhere, even sleeping by my side after chemo treatments. She remains a part of the family today, espe-

cially when the grandchildren are around. I cannot envision my life without her and when my wife Mary is working or not around, I talk to my Rosie all the time.

KEVIN BROPHY

Rosie

MAX

"THIS IS EXACTLY THE kind of dog this place needs!"

So said Stephen Fry at his first sight of Max, our two-year-old springer spaniel.

It was a blustery fall day in 2002. My wife Susanne and I were having tea in the library at Cliveden House in Buckinghamshire. Built on foundations first laid in the 1660s and set on cliffs commanding a view of the River Thames, it had, over its long history, once been home to the Prince of Wales and Lady Nancy Astor. Now it was a luxury hotel. The sort of place where the doorman learned – and remembered – your dog's name.

Back to Stephen Fry. He was there that day for a cast meeting, in the early days of directing his 2003 film, *Bright Young Things*, based on Evelyn Waugh's novel, *Vile Bodies*.

As Fry and his cast hustled into the room, Max was enjoying the plush oriental carpet and the warmth of the hearth, gazing out on the sweeping view of the countryside where he would much rather have been. We were quite happy to linger indoors and eavesdrop on the actors excitedly describing what they would bring to their roles, and Fry gently guiding them toward what he actually wanted.

By this time Max was a far different dog from the shivering wreck that we had first met huddled in a corner at a small animal shelter in North London, having just been abandoned there by his family. We had shown up in search of our next dog, with the vague idea that we wanted to take home a small mongrel, non-shedding female. This dog was none of those things.

But when we entered the room, he deliberately walked over and unhesitatingly sat down on Susanne's feet, looking up at her with pleading chocolate-truffle-brown eyes. Clearly we had a dog. It would be the best 90£ we'd ever spent.

"Springers need lots of exercise," the shelter director had said. In truth, so did we, and so we agreed to venture outside London to properly explore the country we'd been living in for the past six years.

We joined National Trust and English Heritage, followed (then tried in vain to refold) detailed ordnance survey maps and crude footpath signage, explored Stonehenge, traced the path of Hadrian's Wall, and wandered the ruins of Tintern Abbey as an all-male Welsh choir reached notes no man had reached before. We hunted dinosaur fossils on

Dorset's Jurassic Coast as Max hunted rabbits, and we all swam together in Cornwall's Watergate Bay.

There were also adventures much farther afield: longer drives to Montreux, Zürich, Luxembourg, Parma, Sardinia, Paris; and a flight to New York, with Max spending 12 hours in a cage with neither poop nor pee till the tarmac at JFK.

A few years later, we purchased an old stone farmhouse in the Dordogne in France, which became our second home. There, in a forested region famous for truffles and wild boar, neighbors offered to train Max as a hunter-gatherer.

Eventually, there was a new member of the family: a charming and utterly insane female springer puppy we named Montana. We got her as a companion for Max during his golden years, after an attempt to stud him out had failed ("It's probably him," our vet had had said. "Females are so fertile that all you have to do is wave some sperm at them and they get pregnant.") Initially, Max was less than thrilled. She's bat-shit crazy, his look seemed to say, as Montana ambushed him on walks – though later falling sound asleep on top of him. Then, one night in a hotel courtyard in Pisa, she won him over. Two months later, she gave him, and us, 11 puppies.

As is the case for any good conversationalist, Max could

say much by saying very little. A raised eyebrow, a tilt of the head, a tail wag. And a toothy smile that never inspired fear. Did he realize, as Diane Keaton once pointed out in Woody Allen's *Sleeper*, that god spelled backward is dog?

"So, what's your point?" he seemed to say with a tilt of his head.

"Max – you're getting on. Do you know how old you are in dog years?"

"Dogs don't have years," his wag seemed to say. "We live for the day – it makes it easier to manage expectations. You should give it a try."

Dogs are known for their obedience: if you can figure out a way to tell them what to do, they will figure out a way to do it. But in the end, Max decided to disobey our quite clear instructions that he should live forever. Although for more months than we deserved, he fought against the dying of his light, finally, in the warm winter of his sixteenth year, on New Year's Eve, 2015, he died. "Sorry," he seemed to say. "Please take good care of my family." And with a wag and a twitch, he passed into memory.

And then some. Max is survived by the inimitable Montana. In addition to their 11 children, there have been five grandchildren and five great-grandchildren, an extended tribe who found homes stretching from Cornwall to

Cambridge to Kent in the UK, and Sarlat la Canéda in France. A total of 21 bright lights making this corner of the world a better place.

As dogs do, Max also left behind many thousands of wonderful memories for his friends, admirers, and, of course, us. Those memories are mixed with the warm sadness of having loved and been loved unconditionally in return. The arithmetic of having a dog is unforgiving: either we live too long, or they not long enough. The equation rarely balances.

Today, as we travel about with our four generations of remarkably similar liver-and-white springers, aged from 12 years to 15 months, we attract a fair amount of attention.

"Look – twins! Wait – there's three! No – four!" people

say in wonder. "They look so much alike," and "Are they all related?" and, sometimes, "Are you crazy?"

"Well," I say, "it's a long story. It started with a dog called Max."

STEVE BRADY

Max

MEIKO

WHEN WE FIRST MET Meiko, my two very young children and I knew he was a perfect fit. The only trouble was that Meiko (then Morgan) belonged to another family. As luck would have it, his groomer lived across the street from our home, and we just happened to meet him on his first visit. It really was love at first sight!

Meiko is a golden-coloured Shih Tzu-Lassa Apso mix with a touch of Pekinese which makes him look like a cuddly Ewok. His inner spirit oozes with kind, playful happiness. The kids and I fell in love with this 9-month-old "old soul."

As always, life throws all kinds of unexpected surprises your way, some of which can be very trying as they upset your own expectations of what life should be like. This time, however, the curveball landed smack on the bat's sweet spot. A few months later, we learned Meiko had to be removed from his owners due to abuse and the breeder asked us if we'd like to adopt him. We were thrilled and eagerly welcomed Meiko into our home. We inherited Meiko when he was just nine months old, and fifteen years later, he still brings us and many others joy. He is slowing down, though. No longer is he able to jump straight up in the air to get onto my bed – an acrobatic feat for his size, which led to his nickname, Popcorn. Despite having his pelvic basin broken in seven places after a car accident at the age of one, being stone deaf, and somewhat blind, Meiko still brings warmth and laughter everywhere he goes. We go for a two kilometer walk daily, during which we invariably meet our regular band of dog walkers, as well as new people who smile or giggle as Meiko approaches (he looks like he is smiling at them as he waggles forward with his little tongue sticking out just a bit – his blond hair blowing in the wind.)

My dog has shown me that life is good, no matter what obstacles might stand in your way. All it takes is being pres-

ent in the moment, smiling, and spreading your warmth to whoever is heading your way.

JOAN KEARVEL

Meiko

SIENNA

SIENNA WAS ONLY 7 months old when Leo and I adopted her. We got her about a year after we moved in together, and she was our first dog. I'm not completely sure of her background but we were told she found herself at the local shelter as the result of a nasty divorce. Unfortunately, she was the victim. We were told she was a full-blooded golden retriever, but later we suspected that was not the case. Although she was very friendly during our visits to the shelter, she became a bit more timid when things got real. I remember her trembling the day we attempted to take her home. We ended up carrying her out of the shelter because she was too timid to actually cross the threshold. Once we got her home, it wasn't long before she warmed up to us and her new digs. She loved stuffed animals. She used to carry them around constantly and mother them. One time we were hanging out with the neighbors and their dog in our back yard when we noticed that Sienna had disappeared. A brief search found her inside their house where she had piled up all of their dog's stuffed animals into a corner. She was the possessive type when it came to furry friends. She also had a bit of a dominant streak that came out more as she aged. I don't think it was so much a question of an alpha personality as it was that she simply became a cranky old bitch – never with people, not even with young children, but she didn't tolerate antics from other dogs too well, especially younger ones. When we first adopted our Weimaraner Colby, he was 8 months old and Sienna was already about 11 years old. On one of their first evenings together, she had a squeaky toy and he came up and gently took it away from her. She gave him a look as if to say, "I can't believe you just did that. Don't you know who I am?" She gently walked over to him, picked it up and took it back. Once again, he came over and picked it up from her and walked away. She gave the same incredulous look: "Did you just do that to ME?" And again, she gently walked over and took it back from him. A third time he came and attempted to pick it up – that's when she lit into him like there was no tomorrow. She left him with a bloody ear and a lasting reminder that you DO NOT MESS WITH THE BITCH. It was the last time they ever had a disagreement.

She loved to chase things, especially squirrels. She was always going after them, but never with any success of course. But one day when she was in our front yard, she saw a squirrel crossing our driveway. He was solidly on asphalt – no trees to run to – and she was fast. She darted after him, and before he could reach a tree, she actually caught him – at which point the squirrel promptly bit her on the snout and she dropped him fast; he would live to bite another day.

We had to help Sienna across the Rainbow Bridge when she was 13 years and 4 months old – she had stopped eating. They found tumors on her heart and there was internal bleeding.

What did this beautiful girl teach me? She taught that sometimes it's very frightening to take steps away from your known comfy world, but by doing so we can sometimes find a better world than any we could ever have imagined. I'd sure like to think *she* did. She taught me other things too. Watching her catch a squirrel showed me that just because you *can* do something doesn't mean you *should*. And watching her deal with the Weimaraner showed me that you

should always begin with a gentle approach, but then get firm if that's what it takes.

DAVE FLETCHER

Sienna

Grigio

AFTER OUR LHASA DIED, we didn't think we wanted another dog. But when the opportunity presented itself and someone wanted to get rid of a 7-pound Shih Tzu, we were quick to say we would take him.

Dogs have an inner balance in their lives: they don't hold grudges or give the silent treatment – if they love you it does not matter if you are away for ten minutes or ten days, they will enthusiastically greet you. It's also worth noticing the life-balance dogs demonstrate: eat, sleep, play, exercise. If we stay up past our normal bedtime, our dog will look at us and then head off alone to bed! If we forget to put out his food at

Watercolour of Gregio by Master Ken

80

the usual time, he will lock eyes with us until we get it – we forgot to feed him.

Have you ever noticed that when you cough or sneeze, dogs will gaze at you as if to ask, "are you all right?" Our dog loves company and gives equal attention to all our friends, even to the few who are squeamish around dogs.

Right now I see his big eyes looking up at me, saying, it's two thirty, we usually go for a walk at this time. Sorry, time to go!

KEN McALICE

OZ & MOLLY AND ABBY & GRACIE

IN LIFE, DOGS BEFRIEND you as their companions. When they die, they remain etched in your heart forever. Recently our 4-year-old Lab, Oz, died of cancer and then one night a week later, Molly, our 12-year-old Saint Bernard, collapsed, as we say, from a broken heart. We have cried every day as everything we do holds a memory of them. Our house has been so still and so quiet. No eyes looking out the window waiting or tails wagging when we get home. No crazy runs in the yard. No one to tell our secrets to. Can we love another again? Do we want to feel that pain of loss again? Will another even be able to steal our heart?

Oz and Molly

After three months of looking back, we were ready to move forward with their memories. For they taught us how to play, laugh, and love. We will never replace their love but now we are ready to share it with another dog. Recently, Abby called us to be her companion, and with the love of Oz and Molly in our broken hearts she is helping us mend. She has brought happiness back to our house.

Abby was bought from a reputable breeder in California. End of story? No. I called the breeder to find out how she was affected by the devastating California wildfires. During the conversation he mentioned that Abby's little sister had been inadvertently sold to a puppy mill owner and had been bred. The breeder in California had been alerted by the American Kennel Club and she was looking for a new home for her. Well, you guessed it. Gracie is now living with her

sister Abby and she has slowly adapted to a dog-loving home after her life in a crate.

DOUG CLARKE

Abby and Grace

Nellie

Nellie, our precious boxer, was a rescue from a puppy mill seizure in the Eastern Townships area of Quebec where she had spent years in a filthy cage in an unheated, dark barn, where she was bred mercilessly. Given her dreadful condition, she was slated to be euthanized – but her life was spared when, upon examination, it was revealed that she was carrying yet another litter of puppies. Sadly, none of the puppies survived, but Nellie did, just barely – and at approximately 7 or 8 years of age, she crept, tail between her legs, into our lives, and oh so instantly into our hearts. She came to us skeletal, with extreme mange, loss of her ear tips, tail damage due to frostbite, deep sores over much of her body, and fearful of almost everything – including grass and toys. Her upper and lower teeth at the front had been ground down almost to the gum-line and our vet told us that it was likely due to the fact that she had chewed on the metal bars of her prison to keep herself occupied. She also ground what few teeth she had left incessantly for the first 6 months that we had her – another sign of extreme stress, and she suffered from terrifying nightmares that first year that no amount of soothing could lessen. What unspeakable horrors had our Nellie endured in that puppy mill those many years? What was she telling us – and needing to purge herself of? Thank goodness we had Sidney – our big softie rescued mutt with whom she bonded immediately. She found comfort in being close to him and they quickly became inseparable. It was Sidney who taught her that grass was fun to roll in, and how to play with toys – and that her new mums could be trusted. Nellie might have come to us damaged and fearful – but she also came to us with a heart as big as a house – and the most forgiving, loyal, and loving of natures.

After Nellie had been with us about a year, friends of ours, tasked with caring for the livestock of a small farm nearby while the owners were away, asked us if we could help out by conducting a quick check of the farm while they ran errands. It was a bitterly cold day in late winter. At the farm, we spent some time in a freezing barn watching baby lambs at play. After several minutes we became aware of a small form lying motionless on the ground. Closer inspection revealed a tiny, newborn lamb – seemingly abandoned, frozen stiff as a board, and appearing lifeless. As we hovered over it in consternation, we noticed a flutter of movement – so small that it could have been mere wishful thinking – but it galvanized us into action. Isabelle, my partner, sprinted for the car as I scooped up the tiny frozen body and placed it under my winter coat and against my skin. Once in the car with the heater turned up high, we drove at breakneck speed to a sheep farm we knew several kilometers away. I wept the entire way, which Isabelle informed me was of no help whatsoever. One look at the lamb and the farmer shook his head and told us it probably wouldn't survive the 15 minutes it would take to get it home. He gave us frozen colostrum from his supply and waved us off.

Once home we hurriedly wrapped the lamb in some towels – and please don't judge us too unkindly for this – we placed the lamb in the oven with the heat on low and the door open (we subsequently learned that it is best to submerge frozen lambs in warm water). Sidney showed some initial interest, but after being shooed away, kept a respectful distance. Nellie, however, was another matter. She simply would not stop trying to get at the lamb – pawing at us as we stood guard at the oven door. She became so agitated when the lamb began to show signs of life that we attached her leash and secured her to a table-leg. When I think back to our reaction now, I cannot fathom why we ever thought that Nellie would try to harm the lamb. She had never demonstrated anything other than gentleness.

Isabelle then set up a cage in the living room near the wood-burning stove, in readiness for the lamb. First though – the farmer had told us that if the lamb survived it would be imperative to get the colostrum into it. Speaking of the farmer, he knocked on our door about 30 minutes into the rescue operation, armed with more milk and a needle for some sort of necessary shot I cannot recall the name of. He was surprised but gruffly happy the lamb was alive and told us it was a ram. Then, he administered the shot and left, but not before promising to keep us in milk, while also mentioning that it would not be adopted by one of his ewes, and that we would have to be its mother for the next few weeks. As we struggled to get the life-giving colostrum by the dropper full down the lamb's throat, Nellie, in her frantic attempts to get to the lamb, managed to slip her collar off and approached the cage. As we were both close and could have intercepted instantly, we let her approach the lamb. She started by licking its head, thoroughly and none too gently – and then, literally pushing us aside, she entered the cage and proceeded to lick that lamb from stem to stern. Once that job had been accomplished, she settled down next to the lamb, who nuzzled into her and started to accept the milk from the dropper.

Nellie barely left Champ's side for the next three weeks. She would venture outside to do her business in record time, insisted on being fed in the cage, kept Sidney away with warning growls, and became the most wonderful surrogate mother to Champ. Of course she did, because if there was one thing Nellie knew, it was motherhood.

Champ eventually left for his life on the farm – and several months later we visited him. We took Nellie along. Champ had been placed in a fenced enclosure for our meeting and, as we approached, his head went up and he made a beeline for Nellie, bleating loudly. They touched noses and breathed noisily into one another's faces for some time – respective tails wiggling like mad. They then spent time playing and cavorting happily together. When we left, Nellie did not seem fazed and she did not look back. We did not bring Nellie to see Champ again. His life on the farm was good and he was well-cared for, and I like to think Nellie had that all figured out.

I think often of our sweet Nellie, who left us in May of 2017. She lived to be around 15 – which is a long life for a Boxer, especially given her history. Our vet called her our "miracle-Boxer" but to me, Nellie was my very own miracle worker. She cared for her humans with an unwavering dedication and loyalty – and she helped see me through a sorrow in my personal life from which I thought I might never emerge. She cared for me just as she had Champ, never leaving my side. People who love you do their best with words – it is how, full of kind intention, they try to help you find happiness and purpose again, to return to being the same person they knew. But words could not penetrate the dreadful darkness I inhabited. It was Nellie, my silent, patient shadow who, barely leaving my side month after bleak month, reached my battered soul and touched it with her palpable, silent, steadfast presence. It was Nellie, demanding nothing in return, never finding my journey overly prolonged, accepting and loving me even though I was not, and never could be the same. It was Nellie who brought me back.

FIONA BENSON

Champ and Nellie

Part III

Saintly Companions

*If there are no dogs in Heaven, then when
I die I want to go where they went.*

Will Rogers

WHILE CONDUCTING RESEARCH for this book I was curious to know if the saints had any special relationships with "man's best friend." I knew that Saint John Bosco and Saint Francis of Assisi had special relationships with dogs as well as with the dog's relative, the wolf, but somewhat to my surprise I discovered that several other saints had also experienced particularly enriching relationships with dogs. This should have come as no surprise, but unfortunately theological reflections about God's non-human creatures and our relation to them is still more or less in its infancy. Perhaps the close relationship so many of us have with dogs might facilitate our consideration of all animals as worthy of respect and care. To quote theologian Andrew Linzey:

> Animals are not just machines, commodities, tools, resources, utilities here for us, or means to human ends; rather they are God-given sentient beings of worth, value and dignity in their own right. This is a moral and spiritual discovery as objective and as important as any other fundamental discovery, whether it be the discovery of stars and planets or the discovery of the human psyche. One day, theologians will be altogether astonished that it took us so long to see so little.[21]

In his encyclical letter on the environment, *Laudato Si*, Pope Francis outlines the respect one should have for God's creatures: "Teach us (Lord) ... to recognize that we are profoundly united with every creature as we journey towards your infinite light."[22]

As I mentioned previously, at the age of 14 I left home for Ipswich Massachusetts and completed grades 10, 11, and 12 in a junior seminary with the intention of becoming a priest in the Salesian Congregation. Pets were out of the question in the seminary even though Don Bosco, also known as Saint John Bosco, the founder of the congregation, wrote of his experience with a mysterious dog called Grigio (*Grey* in Italian) who seemed to appear out of nowhere when he needed protection. Don Bosco wrote about Grigio in his memoirs, and these were stories that we were very familiar with as Salesian seminarians. We did not doubt the veracity of the story about Grigio because Don Bosco wrote about him in his autobiography and referred to his text as "pure truth." Now, many years later, I still have no doubt about the veracity of the Saint's text, which I have included here in its entirety:

"The grey dog was the topic of many conversations and various conjectures. Many of you have seen him. Now laying aside the fantastic stories which are told of the dog, I will tell you plainly only what is pure truth.

"The frequent attacks which had been made against me made it inadvisable for me to walk to or from the city of Turin alone. In those days, the asylum was the last building on the way to the Oratory. The rest of the way was land covered with hawthorn and acacia trees.

"One dark evening, rather late, I was making my way home with some trepidation when a huge dog appeared beside me, which at first sight gave me a start. But it seemed friendly and even nuzzled me as if I were his master. We quickly became friends, and he accompanied me as far as the Oratory. Many other times that evening's experience was repeated. Indeed, I may say that Grigio did me valuable service. Here are a few examples.

"On a wet, foggy night at the end of November 1854, I was coming from the city. So as not to have a long way to go alone, I took the street connecting Our Lady of Consolation and the Cottolengo. At one point along the street I noticed two men walking a little in front of me. They matched their pace to mine, quickening or slowing down as I did. When I crossed the road to dodge them, they crossed right over in front of me. I attempted to turn back but was not in time. For they suddenly jumped me from behind, keeping an ominous silence, and threw a cloak over my head. I fought to keep from getting tangled up but it was no use. Then one also tried to stuff a rag into my mouth. I was trying to shout but could no longer do so. At that moment Grigio appeared and growling like a bear he leapt into the face of one man while snapping viciously at the other. They plainly would have to tangle with the dog before finishing with me.

"Call off your dog," they began to cry, trembling with fear.

"I'll call him off," I said, "when you agree to leave passersby alone."

"Call him off quick," they exclaimed.

Grigio continued growling liked an enraged wolf or bear. The two men took to their heels, and Grigio stayed by my side, accompanying me until I went to the Cottolengo Institute. After recovering from my scare and refreshed by a drink which that charitable institute always seems to come with at the right moment, I went home with a good escort.

"Every evening when I had no other company, as I passed the last buildings I would see Grigio bound out of nowhere along the way. Many times the Oratory boys saw him. Once he was the centre of an amusing incident. The boys saw him coming into the courtyard. Some wanted to strike him, and others wanted to throw stones at him.

"Don't tease him," Joseph Buzzetti ordered. "That's Don

Bosco's dog." They turned to patting and stroking him then as they brought him along to me. I was in the refectory having supper with some seminarians and priests and with my mother. They were alarmed at the unexpected sight of the dog.

"There's no need to be afraid," I said. "It's my Grigio. Let him come in."

In fact he made a wide tour round the table and came joyfully up to me. I patted him too and offered him some soup, bread, and meat, but he refused all of it. He would not even sniff at what I offered.

"Well, what do you want?" I asked. He only cocked his ears and wagged his tail.

"Either eat or drink or otherwise entertain me," I concluded. He continued to evidence contentment, resting his head on my napkin as if he wanted to speak to me and tell me "Good night." Then the boys, wondering a great deal and quite happy, led him outside.

"The last time I saw Grigio was in 1866 while I was going from Murialdo to Moncucco to see my friend Louis Moglia. The parish priest of Buttigliera wanted to accompany me part of the way, and as a consequence I was surprised by nightfall only halfway on my journey.

"Oh, if only I had my Grigio," I thought to myself, "how

fortunate I would be!" Having said that, I started across a field to take advantage of the last rays of light. Just then Grigio came bounding up to me, full of affection. He accompanied me for the stretch of road that I still had to travel, which was two miles.

"When I got to my friend's house, where I was expected, they asked me to go around another way, fearing there would be a fight between my Grigio and the family's two mastiffs. "If they got into a fight," said Moglia, "they would tear each other to pieces." I talked a lot with the whole family before we sat down to supper. My companion was left to rest in a corner of the room. When we had finished our meal, my friend said, "We must also give Grigio his supper. "He took a little food to bring to the dog; he looked in every corner of the room and of the house, but Grigio was not to be found. We all wondered, since neither door nor window was open, nor had the family dogs given any sign of his departure. We renewed our search upstairs, but no one could find him.

"That is the last news I had of the grey dog that was the subject of so much enquiry and discussion. I never was able to find out who was his owner. I only know that the animal was truly providential for me on many occasions when I found myself in danger."[23]

Don Bosco and Grigio

It was general knowledge to Catholics that St. Francis loved animals and was able to communicate with them in a way that was very unique. Fittingly, the Catholic church made him the patron saint of animals. In a text on the life of St. Francis written at the end of the 14th century, the *Fioretti di San Francesco* (The Little Flowers of St. Francis), one chapter describes Francis' encounter with a wolf – the dog's ancestor. The scientific name for a dog is *canis lupus familiaris,* and it just so happens that wolves and dogs share 98.8% of their DNA. The *Fioretti* tells the story of a wolf in

Gubbio, Italy that attacked animals and humans alike. The townspeople were terrified of the wolf and never ventured beyond the city walls for fear of being killed. Despite the warnings of the people, Francis decided to go and meet the wolf. From a distance the townspeople witnessed the wolf run toward Francis, ready to attack. Francis responded, "Come hither, brother wolf; I command thee, in the name of Christ, neither to harm me nor anybody else."[24] To the surprise of all, the wolf stopped its attack and lay peaceably at Francis' feet. And just as he was known for his special gift of intimacy with nature, even to the point of preaching to the birds, he now preached to the wolf about the terror he was causing among animals and humans alike. He then proposed a peace treaty wherein all would be safe. With his body language, the wolf demonstrated that he agreed with Francis' peace proposal. The townspeople too agreed that for their part they would not try to kill the wolf and even agreed to offer him food when he was hungry. The peace treaty lasted until the death of the wolf two years later. The beast that had been the terror of the region was mourned by the people when he died.[25] Although it's difficult to know exactly how long it took human beings to domesticate dogs, Saint Francis seems to have accomplished this in record time!

Monument in Gubbio, Italy of St. Francis and the wolf

Prayer to St. Francis for our pets:

Good St. Francis, you loved all of God's creatures.

To you they were brothers and sisters.

Help us to follow your example

of treating every living thing with kindness.

Saint Francis, Patron Saint of animals,

watch over my pet

and keep my companion safe and healthy.

Amen

I was familiar with the story of Don Bosco and Grigio, as well as the other stories about Francis' ability to communicate with and even preach to God's creatures. I have discovered, however, that these were not the only saints who had a special relationship with dogs. I was not surprised to learn that the Catholic church has a patron saint for dogs because it has a patron saint for almost every place, profession, country, sickness, or situation you can imagine. Some are logical choices, like St. Francis being the patron of animals. In another vein, the reasoning behind having a patron associated with a specific profession may be related to the Gospels. For instance, Saint Matthew, the tax collector, is the patron of accountants; Mary Magdalene who reputedly washed the feet of Jesus with scented oils is the patroness of perfumers; and Joseph of Arimathea, who offered a tomb for Jesus' burial, is the patron of undertakers. Usually there is a connection, however remote. Saint Joseph of Cupertino apparently levitated during prayer and became the patron of astronauts (and pilots). I'm not quite sure why Saint Anthony the abbot became the patron of gravediggers, or why Saint Fiacre is the patron saint of venereal disease!

The patron saint of dogs is Saint Rocco (or Roch) and there *is* a logical connection. Rocco lived during the time of the Black Death in the 14th century. Millions of people died of the plague during this time. After working with the sick in Italy, Rocco contracted the deadly disease. He decided to die alone in the woods so as not to infect anyone. Resigned to die, and without any food, the Saint was greeted by a dog with a loaf of bread in his mouth. The dog returned every day, and miraculously, Rocco recovered, enabling him to return to his work helping the sick and the dying. Saint Rocco became the patron of dogs and is mostly frequently portrayed with a dog offering him bread.[26]

Saint Rocco

Church lore refers to a good number of other saints who, in a variety of ways, had unique relationships with dogs as well. Here are a few examples: Saint Brigid was kind to dogs and there are stories about her caring for and feeding stray dogs. The Peruvian saint, Saint Martin de Porres, loved animals and would tend to them. He cared for a dog, a cat, and a mouse, and they all got along, to the astonishment of his fellow monks. Saint Margaret of Cortona is often portrayed with a dog pulling on her dress. She only became aware that her lover had died when his dog came to her all on its own and led her to the place where his master was murdered. The dog then brought her to church and her conversion to a saintly life began.

Saint Margaret of Cortona
by Giovanni Battista Piazzetta (1682-1754)

Saint Madeleine Sophie Barat, foundress of the Society of the Sacred Heart, (a teaching order of religious women), had a love for animals and on occasion demonstrated concern for the wellbeing of dogs.

Saint Phillip Neri was a vegetarian because of his love of animals. He also had a special relationship with dogs and would ask aristocrats to take them for a walk as a sign of humility.[27]

Saint Dominic is frequently portrayed with a dog. Apparently, the reason behind this is that before he was born, Dominic's mother, who had difficulty conceiving, went on a pilgrimage to the Abbey of Santo Domingo de Silos in Spain in the hopes that this might help her have a child. In a dream, she saw a dog jump from her womb holding a torch, and with it, he set everything around them on fire. Soon after, she and her husband had a son and named him Dominic, after Saint Dominic of Silos. Dominic called his order the Order of Preachers, and members of his order sign O.P. after their names. The order would later come to be known as the Dominicans (in Latin "Dominicanus"), which is very close to "domini canis" or "dog of the Lord." The Order's vocation was to zealously preach the Gospel, so the nickname seemed appropriate, and Dominicans are still referred to as the Hounds of the Lord![28]

Saint Dominic

If you think about it, it's logical to presume that St. Bernards were named with some connection to a saint in mind – in fact, that saint was Saint Bernard of Menthon, a 10th century monk, who, along with his confreres, founded a hospice. The monks trained dogs for protection and to help find lost pilgrims passing through the mountain passes of the Alps on their way to Rome. Eventually, the dogs, the hospice, as well as two mountain passes were named after Saint Bernard of Menthon. These magnificent dogs were also referred to as "Saints' Dogs."[29]

Painting of a monk with St. Bernards
by Salvator Rosa (1615-1673)

MONKS AND THEIR GUARDIAN DOGS

ABOUT FORTY YEARS AGO, I was on a study trip in India and Sri Lanka. When I was in Sri Lanka, I was most fortunate to stay in a Buddhist monastery near the city of Kandy. My sleeping accommodations consisted of a cave – the first and probably last time I will experience cave dwelling. The cave, however, was clean and cool and quite comfortable. During this time, I had the opportunity to eat with the monks and observe their rituals. I noticed that the head monk had a German shepherd – quite a large one. I was curious as to why the monks would have a dog on the premises, but I soon understood. The monastery was situated on the side of a mountain with tropical forest above it. The monks would put out food and other offerings around their shrine of the Buddha, including oil lamps and other decorations. The problem was that rhesus monkeys would come out of the forest and wreak havoc by eating the offerings, knocking over the oil lamps, and making quite a mess. I had already observed the mayhem monkeys could cause in India and the vigilance and effort it took to keep them at a distance. This is where the German shepherd's vigilance was of great help to the monks. He loved to chase monkeys and would take off after them as soon as they were spotted coming down the side of the mountain toward the monastery. At the sight of the dog, the monkeys would scurry back into the forest. It was amusing to see the monkeys cautiously come down the mountain on the lookout for the dog. There seemed to be a leader among them that looked like some old war veteran with a brush cut and a bum arm. I don't know if his injured arm was the result of an encounter with the German shepherd, but whenever the dog was spotted, a general screech could be heard from the monkeys and it was back to the forest for the troupe.

Buddhist Monk with his guardian of the temple

I have also observed dogs working as guardians for monks much closer to my home. The monks in question are members of the Cistercian order and their monastery in rural Quebec is a brief drive from where I live. I have had opportunities over the years to spend time with the monks and it has always been an enriching experience. I stay for a few days at a time and take advantage of my opportunity to get caught up on work and soak up the peace and quiet of the community. The monks have an impressive 40-acre apple and pear orchard which provides them with their main source of income. In the fall season, hundreds gather (including my family) to pick these apples and pears. Early on however, the monks realized that the over-population of deer in the area would be a problem. The deer, who have no natural predators in the area, were a problem not because they ate too many apples, but because they ate the bark off the saplings, which in turn resulted in the trees dying. The monks tried a variety of different tactics to keep the deer away. Fences didn't work, as the deer simply jumped over them. The monks would, of course, never have considered any solution that would directly hurt or kill the deer, but the livelihood of the monastery was at stake. After some consultation, they decided to get a pack of huskies and, voilà, their problem was solved. Today, the dogs have the run of the orchard and their presence keeps the deer away. The huskies are friendly and not to be feared by visitors to the orchard. However, during apple picking season, they are kept separate from the apple pickers, as some people bring their dogs to the orchard. Their food includes table scraps from visitors who stay at the monastery, and even though they have shelters, I have seen them on many a bitter cold winter night curled up outside with their noses tucked into their fur. Once, watching one of them get up, I noticed that the snow and ice had melted underneath him. These are tough dogs made for Canadian winters. Some of the dogs are bred occasionally and provide renewal for the pack, while others are sold to would-be husky companions. I asked one of the monks, Father Jacques, to write something about the dogs and he kindly obliged. He started out by explaining the need to protect the orchard from the deer and the solution the pack of huskies had provided and went on to elaborate on the strict hierarchy among the dogs. The alpha male and alpha female have priority when it comes to food, lodging, mating, and even a caress from a human. Punishment is quick and can be severe, even fatal, if this hierarchy is not respected – much as it is in a wolf pack. Father Jacques always took measures to ensure that the dogs lower down in the hierarchy were allowed to eat before the alpha male and female. He went on to compare the dogs' hierarchy with a common human experience: the domination of the weak by the powerful. His reflection about the huskies led him to deliver a sermonette about our need for conversion regarding our relationship with the marginalized:

Our first instinct is to always prioritize those we consider best. We tend to be interested in people who are prominent in society and we tend to neglect those who are handicapped, poor, and boring. This law of the jungle governs our relations between people, between groups or social classes, and our international relations. Mercilessly, the powerful monopolize for themselves all possible benefits while exploiting the weakest among them.

I believe that what Father Jacques was getting at was that we should not behave like a hierarchical pack of huskies. He further pointed out that, "We are invited by Jesus to be inclusive and loving of the weak, the poor, the powerless, the voiceless, and the handicapped." I must admit that I was somewhat taken aback by his text and his sermonette because I was expecting him to focus more on all the dogs have accomplished and less on how their hierarchy is reflected in human society in less-than-desirable ways. Later, in an email to me, Father Jacques wrote, "I'm sorry if I was politically incorrect." Actually I realize now that he was being very morally and politically correct. It is undeniably true that human society also has a hierarchy where the rich and the powerful tend to be neglectful of those who are marginalized. But while the huskies were acting out their intrinsic "survival of the fittest" instincts, humans are *supposed to* have a different sort of moral compass. After thinking about his text, I came to the conclusion that dogs, in a good home, often find themselves in a better environment than when they are in a hierarchical pack with other dogs. I have also observed such a hierarchy among feral dogs in India. Father Jacques had even described how it was a completely different situation for one of their pups after it had been adopted into a family. Some time after receiving his email, I happened to meet Father Jacques during apple picking season in the orchard. We chatted about his text and he reiterated that the monk-husky partnership is a mutually beneficial one. "They are doing what we want them to do," he concluded.

The consistent theme in all of these stories of saints and monks is that dogs have faithfully protected, helped, and guided their saintly companions. This kind of dedication is an indication of true virtue that they continue to gift us with to this day.

Father Joseph with the guardians of the orchard

Part IV

What Dogs Do For Us

You think those dogs will not be in heaven! I tell
you they will be there long before any of us.

Robert Louis Stevenson

IN HER 2008 ARTICLE ENTITLED, "The Healing Power of the Human Animal Interaction," researcher Margo Halm writes:

> As long ago as 1860, Florence Nightingale commented that, "A small pet is often an excellent companion for the sick, for long chronic cases especially." More than 100 years later, the immediate and long-term human health benefits of animals on the mind, body, and spirit continue to be documented. Effects of animal assisted therapy (AAT) are primarily attributed to 'contact comfort', a tactile process whereby unconditional attachment bonds form between animals and humans, inducing relaxation by reducing cardiovascular reactivity to stress.[30]

Research on the human-animal bond has implications for health care professionals which go beyond clinical practice. As psychology professor and dog expert Stanley Coren points out, "Children with communication difficulties, adults with social inter-action or depressive problems, and the elderly suffering from isolation and loneliness have all been helped by the presence of companion dogs."[31] Numerous scholarly articles have also been published regarding

the diverse physical and mental health benefits of pet ownership or access to pet therapy. More empirical studies are
required, but, as Marguerite O'Haire put it in her article
"Companion animals and human health: Benefits, challenges, and the road ahead," owning a dog is a "healthy
choice."[32]

Evidence of the positive psychological effects of a dog's
presence has been made known by Companions for Courage, an association located in central Florida. The State allows a child to be accompanied in court "to enable the Court
to establish conditions it finds just and appropriate when
taking the testimony of a child, including the use of a therapy animal ..."[33] That is what Karl, a five-year-old boxer does.
As a companion for Courage, he accompanies children who
have to testify in court about their experiences of physical
and sexual abuse. Karl and many other dogs have provided
a calming and reassuring presence for children dealing
with such trauma.[34]

The use of dogs in such situations is more and more
common. A provincial police dog in Quebec known as
Sundae had a particularly calming effect on a six-year-old
girl who was then able to testify about being a victim of
abuse. The policeman said that it was the dog that made
the difference, ultimately making the trial possible.[35]

Research has shown that pet therapy for hospitalized psychiatric patients can be very beneficial. In one study by Barker and Dawson, entitled, "The Effects of Animal-Assisted Therapy on Anxiety Ratings of Hospitalized Psychiatric Patients." they conclude. "Among patients who participated in animal-assisted therapy, patients with mood disorders, psychotic disorders, and other disorders had a significant mean decrease in anxiety."[36] I need no convincing regarding the beneficial effects of pet therapy on psychiatric patients having seen the joy my Molly brings to them. One patient, a huge Molly fan, had a weekend pass, yet told me that even though she would be allowed to leave, she wanted to spend more time with Molly. Another patient told me that Molly "made her day," and another said, "Molly made me smile and it is not easy for me to smile." When I asked the psychiatrist on the ward what he had observed about Molly and the benefits of pet therapy, he agreed, and sent me this brief text:

> Having Molly visit our patients in the inpatient unit is quite special. For many, she is the only visitor they have. She is non-threatening, non-judgmental, and very respectful. Patients feel it and they show her love and affection. When she shows up, there are smiles and laughter and her energy and good humour radiate as she wags her tail in the hallways. May she and her master continue their good work for a long time.

Other individuals have also personally testified to the beneficial effects of dogs on mental health. Julie Barton is one such individual:

> I'd been recently diagnosed with major depression after a wicked and precipitous collapse, but the moment I held that puppy in my hands, my suicidal ideation stopped and sorrow seemed less immense. I knew it then, and I still believe it fervently: I had found my medicine and it came

in the form of a dog ... His presence, his essence,

his joy, our connection: those things were

my oxygen.[37]

A friend of mine, the late Father Emmet Johns, received the Order of Canada for his work with homeless youth in Montreal. He told me that when he was chaplain at a psychiatric hospital, there was a young patient there who used to run away regularly. At one point, the hospital got a therapy dog for the patients and this young escapee was given the responsibility of taking care of the dog. He never ran away again. Father John's youth center for the homeless also happened to offer veterinary care and food for dogs. He observed that the young, homeless dog owners could eat hot dog after hot dog yet would carefully examine the ingredients on the bags of dog food that were offered. This story illustrates the important role dogs can play in helping to establish some semblance of family life among the most vulnerable, some of whom may have had little chance of joining a human family. Adam Miklosi, a renowned researcher on the study of human-dog interaction, concluded that many homeless people "establish a social relationship by voluntarily adopting a dog."[38]

A study published in the 2016 edition of *Pet Behaviour*

Science reveals that homeless individuals sometimes take on the care of a dog despite the fact that they appear to gain little if any advantage from this relationship and more often the presence of the dog made their lives harder.[39] There is scant evidence that the companionship of these dogs increased donations, although they were reported useful as night guards. There are costs, however, associated with this kind of pet-keeping; homeless dog owners are not usually allowed into community shelters with their animals, and consequently sleep outdoors. Although there does seem to be more sensitivity about this issue in recent years. During a particularly frigid cold spell in Montreal a couple of years ago, extra beds were made available in a former hospital, and individuals could bring their pets. One of the rules was that only one dog could be in the elevator at a time. Why would the homeless undertake the added responsibility of caring for a dog? Miklosi points out that perhaps it's because the presence of dogs can "help reduce loneliness and improve health in the case of the homeless."[40] Interestingly, researcher John Bradshaw, who has studied dogs' behavior and their interactions with people extensively, points out that people are more receptive to the homeless when they have dogs:

Even scruffy or potentially aggressive dogs seem capable of overcoming people's natural reticence when encountering strangers. In one study, a handler was dressed in torn, dirty jeans, scuffed work boots, an old T-shirt, and a stained pea coat. His dog wore a studded collar with a frayed piece of rope for a lead. Nevertheless, passersby were eight times more likely to approach or smile at the handler than when he was on his own.[41]

Dogs can also have a beneficial effect within homeless shelters. In journalist Jesse Feith's article in the Montreal Gazette, "The Dog that helps the homeless in Montreal," he describes howArgon, a service dog, a recent addition at the men's shelter known as *La Maison du Père*, has had positive effects on the residents. The men at the shelter often have limited communication with others, but always seem open to communicating with Argon. "Argon is the best idea this place could have had," one resident shared. "He allows people to create a link, to interact and live a little piece of a normal life. I know he will help a lot of people. He is already helping." One of the workers referred to the difficult histories of so many of the men and how they have been betrayed and marginalized by society. But from Argon, "they only get love."[42]

There is also research showing that owning a dog can improve one's chances of striking up a romantic relationship. I remember my nephew telling me that his dog Chase boosted his possibility of romantic involvement. Indeed, there is actually some evidence that he was correct. Bradshaw refers to a study in France which demonstrates that there is a certain appeal associated with dog owners.

> The ease with which dog owners strike up conversations with one another seems to reflect an aura of trustworthiness endowed by the dog that that owner would not possess if alone. This effect seems remarkably powerful: for example, in one study conducted in France a twenty-year-old male delivered the following chat-up line to 240 young women chosen at random while walking alone in a pedestrian-only area: "Hello, my name's Antoine. I just want to say that I think you're really pretty. I have to go to work this afternoon, but I was wondering if you would give me your phone number. I'll phone you later and we can have a drink together someplace." When Antoine was accompanied by a dog (not his own), almost a

third of the young women handed over their phone numbers; when he was on his own, fewer than 10 percent did so. In another study, adding the phrase "with a dog" to a dating profile of a man clearly interested only in short-term relationships, nevertheless induced some women to rate him as a serious marriage prospect. The power of dogs to draw people into conversation suggests that a facility with animals is intrinsically appealing (even when that facility had been faked).[43]

Simply walking one's dog gives occasion to speak to another dog owner – it has happened to me far too many times to count. When I vacationed in Florida, I chatted with strangers around the neighbourhood simply because we were walking our dogs, and inevitably we would ask about the breed, the name of the dog, his or her age, and so on and so forth. Oftentimes I remembered the dog's name but not the owner's!

Dogs can also improve the life of the incarcerated. The December 2014 edition of *The Economist* featured an article entitled "Pups and perps-what has four legs, a wet nose and helps young thugs grow up?" The article points out the remarkably positive influence of dogs on prisoners, noting, "we have discovered that prisoners often identify with rescue dogs – they both have experienced trauma – and they are eager to become their protectors."[44] The article also points out that working with dogs resulted in a significant reduction in stress and anxiety among prisoners. In her article "The experiences of offenders in a prison canine program," published in *Federal Probation – A Journal of Correctional Philosophy and Practice,* Wendy G. Turner explores the tangible benefits of pairing inmates with dogs:

> While further systematic research and analysis
> are needed, the anecdotal reports from staff,
> inmates, and recipients of the service dogs
> are overwhelmingly positive; therefore, not
> surprisingly, animal training programs are
> becoming increasingly common in correctional
> facilities. The Joseph Harp Correctional Center,
> a medium security prison in Oklahoma,
> implemented a unique canine program,
> pairing depressed inmates with dogs. The
> results showed that, "Not only did the program
> decrease depression among those inmates,
> but the rates of aggression decreased among

the inmates as well."[45]

Another example of a successful dog training program for inmates was the one initiated by Sister Pauline Quinn, an American Dominican nun who suffered abuse as a child but who was able to begin a personal process of healing thanks to a stray German shepherd. She started her first prison dog program in 1981 at the Washington State Correctional Center for Women. The program is described as follows:

> The Oshkosh program, called "Paws Forward," uses inmates to provide obedience training to dogs destined for use as guide dogs for the blind, 'We've found the training program to be good for the inmates and our staff atmosphere,' said OSCI warden Judy Smith. 'A lot of our inmates haven't seen a dog for years. There's something about a pet that changed the atmosphere of the institution.'[46]

Sister Quinn's program has spread to 40 prisons and includes training for service dogs. It also has the benefit of preparing inmates for employment possibilities as dog trainers and groomers. Sister Quinn died in 2020 but her legacy of helping inmates heal through working with dogs lives on.

Dogs can also help to reduce the tension experienced by university students during exam time. In April 2015, McGill University in Montreal invited students to take a "paws" with therapy dogs in the university student center and libraries. Students were invited to:

> Come out to the Brown Building Lobby, on April 24th at 5:00 – 6:30 pm to de-stress with therapeutic dogs. Leave your labs/offices, and Touch, Pet, Play and have fun with wonderful dogs at a convenient, end-of-the-day, time for graduate students. Take care of yourself with wagging tails and lots of licks! Pop in for a few minutes or stay the whole time. Dog treats and toys will be provided [for the dogs that is!][47]

The university website quoted researcher Margo Halm's 2008 article, "The Healing Power of the Human Animal Interaction," in which she described pet therapy as "inducing relaxation by reducing cardiovascular reactivity to stress." Based on her analysis, Halm concluded, "this intervention may contribute to optimal healing environments that promote harmony of mind, body, and spirit."[48]

McGill is not unique in its undertaking of this experiment. John Bradshaw, director of the Anthrozoology Institute based at the University of Bristol in the United Kingdom, describes how, "One group of people almost guaranteed to feel anxious are undergraduate students during examination time. Over 1,000 universities around the world have put so-called animal visitation programs into place to help students calm themselves."[49] It has been documented by a number of researchers that dogs demonstrate the emotional response of empathy towards humans expressing distress.[50]

Scientists tell us that dogs are unique in the animal kingdom because of the way they interact with another species (us) in a way that no other animal does. Indeed, your dog likely prefers to be with you than with another dog. In *Inside of a Dog,* Horowitz calls dogs "canine anthropologists" and points out that they are constantly "reading us." They know things about us that we don't even know ourselves, and they love what they know. I always have the feeling that the minute I move, Molly is reading me. 'What's he up to? Is he going for his shoes and possibly a walk? Did I hear car keys? Why isn't he taking me with him? Is that food I smell? Will he share if I sit nicely? Is he willing to give me a belly rub? I can't get the ball under the sofa and I am looking at him for help. Why isn't he helping me? He's talking to me and I'm trying to figure out what he's saying.' This is a unique characteristic in the relationship between humans and animals. Indeed, only dogs study our faces and make prolonged eye contact with us. They puzzle over our intent (dogs have that special quizzical look indicating their attempt to understand us).[51] It is also quite evident that they also read one another when they encounter each other. One only has to observe their sniffing rituals to know this is true. A gym friend, Richard, when asked for a dog story, shared the following incredible tale:

> I have two dogs, a golden doodle name Sophie, and Yoko, a husky Labrador mix. One day I was giving them their daily treat. Yoko has the habit of gulping down in one bite, while Sophie sets it down and prevents Yoko from stealing it while sometimes taking forever to eat it herself. Note: both dogs have a habit of barking when they see someone in the street. So one day, after I had given them their treats and Yoko had eaten hers, she got up, went to the door, and started barking. As soon as Sophie got up to join in barking at whatever was there, Yoko turned around and stole Sophie's treat. There was no one outside. I figured

that it had to be a coincidence, but no, because I saw her repeat the same trick and my wife also saw her do it multiple times. Not dumb at all.

Amazingly, when people were asked to quantify different aspects of inter-individual family relationships (e.g. companionship, intimacy, conflict, alliance, etc.), they found that by and large, dogs had been integrated into the web of family relations. Human–dog relationships showed higher scores for companionship, nurturance, and reliance than human–human relationships.[52] It reminded me of an article I saw noting that during divorce proceedings, "Who gets the dog?" tends to be a very contentious question, with some couples even settling for joint custody!

It is also a known fact that dog owners usually get significantly more exercise than those who do not have a dog. A doctoral dissertation in Britain concluded that dog owners walked on average 20 minutes more a day than non-dog owners and that the added physical activity was particularly beneficial for older adults. Exercising twenty minutes more may not seem like much, but that adds up to 2 hours and 20 minutes a week – a significant increase, especially when you consider that the research studied the elderly.[53] There are numerous other studies which also show that households with dogs result in a significant increase in exercise for their owners. As John Bradshaw so aptly put it, "... I know from experience that the most reliable prompt for a twice-daily walk is a dog charging around the hallway with his leash in his mouth and his tail in overdrive!"[54] For many, that walk is the best part of the day.

Adrian Raeside demonstrated a deep understanding of this in his very insightful comic, *The Other Coast.*

@raesidecartoon.com

And still others, like columnist Brittany Foster, testify to the simple joy of walking their dog:

> Morning walks with Bernie help give me a fresh start to every day. Our night walks restore my strength when I feel weak or defeated by what the previous hours have thrown at me. Walks with Bernie remind me about the importance of staying physically active, help me appreciate

the beauty around me, and calm my mind and
its racing thoughts.[55]

In addition to their substantial health benefits, dogs also
contribute to society in myriad other ways. They help police
locate missing individuals and aid in intercepting and
preventing illegal drugs and explosives from entering the
country. In a publication celebrating the 75th anniversary
of Montreal's Trudeau Airport, there is an article about the
dogs that work there. They are mostly German shepherds;
however other breeds are also on the job. The publication
outlines the different canine specialties: "Beagles are particularly good at detecting food products, while Labrador
retrievers are excellent drug sniffers."[56] No human or
machine has been able to do a better job at these tasks. In
fact, they are so good at what they do that those who profit
from illegal drugs have occasionally placed ransoms on
dogs who disrupt their trade. For instance, Sombra, a
German shepherd who helped police find thousands of
pounds of cocaine in Columbia consequently had a
$70,000 hit put on her by a drug cartel.[57] There is no indi-
cation that they succeeded.

We are of course aware that dogs are used for therapy,
but may be surprised to discover that there are about

50,000 therapy animals in the United States alone.[58] Among their many acts of service, they forewarn epileptic and diabetic owners of impending seizures.[59] Psychotherapist Dr. Boris Levinson was the first to use the term "pet therapy" after he accidentally discovered that dogs could have a therapeutic effect, especially on non-communicative children:

> As the story goes, one day a mother and her chronically withdrawn son arrived early for their appointment to find that Dr. Levinson had not yet removed his dog, Jingles, from his office. The child, who had never spoken during previous sessions, suddenly began to address the dog and then began to respond to Dr. Levinson's questions, albeit directing his replies not to him but to the dog. Inspired by this success, Levinson began to incorporate Jingles into his treatment of other young patients and found that many happily played with the dog even when they were uncomfortable speaking to him: by gradually insinuating himself into these games, he found that he could establish trust with many of these children. While his academic colleagues were

initially skeptical about using animals in psychotherapy, he energetically promoted his methods, which, by his death in 1984, had become widely accepted in the United States.[60]

There seems to be an endless list of therapeutic benefits connected to owning and interacting with dogs. Research shows, "pet therapy can reduce the agitation of patients suffering from dementia and, as with those suffering from depression, enhance their interactions with their caregivers."[61] Author and artist Maria Kalman in her book *Beloved Dog* does a portrait of a dog named Zoloft, and another individual in the text referred to his dog as an "antidepressant on four legs".[62]

Dogs serve us in many other ways as well. It amazes me that despite all of our advances in technology, there is no machine that can do a better job helping the visually impaired than a dog can.

Dogs have also been trained to detect cancer of the bladder, breast, lung, skin, and prostate. The accuracy with which they can detect prostate cancer is quite amazing, with a success rate of 91%.[63] More recently dogs are being trained in a pilot project in Finland to detect the Covid 19 virus. There also seems no end to the possibilities when it comes to training a dog to detect certain odors. I constantly come across articles about dogs trained to perform a service regarding human health that I had not heard of before. Professional hockey player Max Domi is diabetic, but his dog Orion (thanks to dogs' incredible sense of smell), can detect a lack of sugar in his master's saliva and will alert him when there is a dangerous variation.[64] "*Medical alert dogs* have been used to recognize and alert humans to changes that occur before symptoms become evident. Patients with epilepsy, Addison's disease, diabetes, migraines, anxiety disorders, and other medical conditions have all benefited from health alerts provided by dogs."[65]

There seems no end to the power of a dog's nose. One dog trainer was asked if he could train dogs to detect bedbugs. He was quite surprised since he had trained dogs to do many things, but he had never been asked to train them to sniff out bugs. He succeeded, however, and one of his dogs, a terrier, was able to check out 80 hotel rooms a day, discovering that 8% of the rooms had bedbugs. The accuracy rate for dogs detecting bedbugs is 97%.[66] The May 28th, 2011 edition of the Washington Post reported, "Demand for bedbug-sniffing dogs skyrocketing." This service is now widely available.

A dog's sense of smell can be up to 100,000 times more powerful than a human's. It still amazes me when, all of a sudden, Molly jumps up from her sleep and starts barking at the back door. When I look out, I see a cat walking at the back of my property about 60 yards away! In her book, *Being a Dog: Following the Dog into a World of Smell*, Alexandra Horowitz best sums up dogs' incredible noses and what they do for us:

> Detection dogs have been trained to find just
> about anything, from the lock to the stock
> and barrel. Dogs find, we know, explosives,
> accelerants, and landmines. They find missing
> people, still alive – and cadavers, on land or
> underwater. They can smell out drugs and
> counterfeit goods. But they can also detect illicit
> cell phones in prison and imported sharks' fin
> in suitcases; termites, fire ants, and the red
> palm weevil, which kills palm trees used both

ornamentally and for their dates; screwworm, nematodes, and bedbugs; invasive knapweed in Montana and invasive brown tree snakes in Guam; the hard-to-spot Northern white whale in the sea and the Amur tiger on land; the feces of black bears, fishers, bobcats, maned wolves, bush dogs, and turtles; birds killed on wind farms and dairy cows who have come into estrus. Provided that it has an odor, it can be smelled out by a dog. There are now dogs put into service to find other, lost dogs.[67]

Here is a recap of just a few things dogs do for us (incomplete, to be sure):

- Improve our physical health
- Improve our mental health
- Improve our emotional state
- Improve our mobility
- Protect our property
- Help the disabled
- Find missing people
- Sniff out drugs, explosives, bedbugs, and invasive species
- Detect cancer cells, and other life threatening conditions

Part V

What Dogs Teach Us

*The average dog is a nicer person
than the average person.*

Andy Rooney

IN AN INTERVIEW, psychology professor Alexandra Horowitz discussed how we can learn a lot about ourselves by studying and observing dogs. I believe that our relationship with them can help bring out the best in us and teach us many valuable lessons. Here are five such lessons:

BE GRATEFUL

MOST FAMILIES WILL outlive their dogs. For many children it is very traumatic when they first experience the death of what many people refer to as a member of the family. When my nephew Rick, a middle-school teacher in Oregon, would ask his students about the members of their families at the beginning of the school year, he told me that they would always include their dogs. The death of a dog may be expected, like it was with Teddy, or a complete shock, as it was with Curly and Monty. When my mother died just after my 11th birthday, it was a shock and I'm not sure if I've gotten over it to this day. I took for granted that her love and presence would be around for a lot longer. Dogs likewise teach us that life is short and that we should cherish and be grateful for the time we have with one another. For children, the loss of the family dog can be worse than the loss of a family member that they do not see very often or know very well. As author Jeffrey Moussaieff Masson so aptly put it, "It just doesn't seem fair that they have such short life spans. True, they live their twelve-odd years with such intensity that it really is like living to eighty-four. Still, they leave such a hole in our lives."[68] As I have already recalled, when we finally decided to bring Teddy to the veterinarian to be euthanized, the whole family was sobbing in the car on our way to his office. As novelist T.H. White notes, unlike many relatives, when it comes to dogs, "you love them most at last."[69] I wanted my children to recall and be grateful for the memories of Teddy greeting them first thing in the morning and his joy in welcoming them after school. Parents certainly can help their grieving children by recalling all the good times their dog brought them – from the time they were a puppy (or from the time they came into the home) until the very end – and the importance of being grateful for all those wonderful stories that will be remembered forever.

Brother David Steindl-Rast, a Benedictine monk, is renowned for his reflections on gratitude. He famously said, "The root of joy is gratefulness ... It is not joy that makes us grateful; it is gratitude that makes us joyful."[70] Dogs seem to have gratitude and joy all wrapped up in one package. Saint Basil pondered, "Does not the gratitude of the dog put to shame any man who is ungrateful to his bene-factors?"[71] The mere mention of a walk sets off a grateful joy expressed by tail wagging that at times moves the dog's whole posterior. Even when my brother started to spell the word "walk" it did not take long for his dog Tess to figure out what the word meant, and her grateful joy would kick in. Dogs know how to express joy even when they are very sick or injured. I will always remember my Curly, looking at me and attempting to wag his tail after he had been hit by a truck. Our dogs are always grateful and joyful when we get home. As my friend Ken shared in his story about his dog Grigio, "If they love you it does not matter if you are away for ten minutes or ten days, they will enthusiastically greet you." A Florida family expressed their gratitude for their dog Marty (2002-2018) in an obituary in a local Catholic newspaper: "You taught us how to live and love one's life and how to love others unconditionally. We thank God for blessing us with our time with you!"[72] This gratitude for our dogs, and dogs in general, is so evident. Indeed, "We are grateful for the very existence of dogs, and I like to think that they feel the same way about us. Both species have a lot to be grateful for. It is one of the great miracles of nature that we have come together in love and friendship in a way that no other two species ever have."[73] To be sure, humans and dogs have always had and will undoubtedly continue to have a mutually beneficial relationship.

CARPE DIEM – LIVE IN THE PRESENT

ROBIN WILLIAMS, in the film *Dead Poets Society*, helped to popularize the expression "Carpe diem" (often translated as "Seize the day") by sensitizing his students to the importance of living in the moment. When we use this expression, we usually mean to say: enjoy the moment, because who knows what awaits us? The expression originated over 2000 years ago with the Latin poet Horace:

> *sapias, vina liques et spatio brevi*
> *spem longam reseces. dum loquimur, fugerit invida*
> *aetas: carpe diem quam minimum credula postero.*
> *Be wise, strain the wine, and cut back hope for a long*
> *life in a short time. Even as we speak, this envious*
> *lifetime is fleeing: seize the day, trusting as little*
> *as possible to the next.*

The French philosopher and mathematician Blaise Pascal wrote: "I have discovered that all of man's unhappiness comes from one thing, not knowing how to rest peacefully in a room." Although many spiritual masters, be they

Christian, Hindu or Buddhist, teach us that gratefully living in the moment is the best way to experience peace, it's not always easy for us to be present. Posters announcing mindfulness teaching sessions are often seen in hospitals; universities; and in myriad other places, giving the impression that humans have discovered something new. Yet the notions of mindfulness and meditation were taught by the Buddha 2500 years ago. Buddhist scholar Bukkyō Dendō Kyōkai wrote, "The secret of health for both mind and body is not to mourn for the past, nor to worry about the future, but to live the present moment wisely and earnestly."[74] Modern psychology delivers the same message: avoid dwelling in the past or the future, as the only time we really have is *now*. In his seminal work about the hierarchy of needs, highly respected psychologist Abraham Maslow writes, "The ability to be in the present moment is a major component of mental wellness."[75] As Emily Dickinson so aptly wrote, "Forever is composed of nows."[76] Dogs live in the now. That's all they seem to know. Remember what Max said to this master when he was asked, "Do you know how old you are in dog years?" He wag-smiled, "Dogs don't have years. We live for the day – it makes it easier to manage expectations." In his bestselling book *Marley and Me: Life and Love with the World's Worst Dog*, John Grogan relates:

"Marley taught me about living each day with unbridled exuberance and joy, about seizing the moment and following your heart. He taught me to appreciate the simple things – a walk in the woods, a fresh snowfall, a nap in a shaft of winter sunlight."[77] I recall being on the beach in Boca Raton, Florida, early in the morning – when dogs can still roam freely. As the sun was rising over the ocean, the dogs were exuberant in their joy – running in and out of the surf, rolling in the sand, chasing balls and each other. Then I spotted many of their masters, walking along the beach staring down at their phones, oblivious to their surroundings. The dogs got it right.

Mindfulness, meditation, and living in the now are all approaches to stopping and resting our busy, worried minds – minds which, in Hinduism, have been compared to a tree full of scampering monkeys – and immersing ourselves in the peaceful present. I have discovered that not only do dogs live in the present, but they help us do the same. Dogs have a calming effect on us simply by being present. Humourist Dave Barry writes seriously about a lesson he learned from his dog Lucy:

> But what I really admire about Lucy's mindfulness
> ... is the way it enables her to be such a wonderful

companion. It's a cliché, but only because it is so obviously true: *nobody loves you the way your dog loves you.* When you're with your dog, you may be mentally elsewhere, but your dog is not; your dog is always right there with you. When you're gone, your dog is waiting for you to come back, so it can be with you again. Because being with you makes your dog happier than anything else.[78]

The very touching stories by my friends about Annie and Rosie are powerful examples of how important and therapeutic a dog's presence can be. About her dog, Margaret Mead said to a friend, "He rests me."[79] Several renowned authors, both past and present, have also iterated the power of the present moment. "Realize deeply that the present moment is all you have. Make the NOW the primary focus of your life,"[80] writes Eckhart Tolle in his best seller, *The Power of Now.* Centuries earlier, the philosopher and scientist Sir Francis Bacon (1561-1626) described this truth beautifully. I came across his words when visiting the Monterey Aquarium in California: "We have only this moment, sparkling like a star in our hand and melting like a snowflake." Anne-Marie Trepanier, our dog trainer, has also eloquently described how dogs have mastered the art of living in the present moment:

> Living in the present moment is one of the things
> I learned from my dogs. The dog does not think
> about yesterday or tomorrow – when he eats, he is
> focused on eating, when he explores, he smells
> and analyzes, when he plays with us, he does not
> think about anything else. I started to focus on the
> moments that I spend with my dogs instead of
> thinking about other things.

Many authors have expressed how important it is not to let worry, guilt, or preoccupation with what we in the seminary called "worldly matters" rob us of the joy inherent in the present moment. I think of the time I spend with my grandchildren and how everything else takes a back seat to those precious times. They too, teach me that what we are doing now is all we need to do or think about doing.

In *The Five Secrets You Must Discover Before You Die,* John Izzo asked people over the age of 60 to identify the secrets to their happiness. One of these, unsurprisingly, is: live in the moment. While Izzo learned this from the wise people he interviewed, he also realized that he could have learned this from his dog as well:

In this regard, my dog has been one of my best teachers. Each day when I'm not travelling, my dog Molly and I take a walk up the side of the mountain where we live. For 40 minutes we walked straight up and then walk back down. After taking these walks for several years I came to an interesting realization. My dog was enjoying our walks far more than I was! For me, the goal was simply to get to the top of the mountain and come back down. The walk was not to be savoured but to be gotten through. I was walking in order to get exercise and hopefully to live a longer life rather than seeing the walks as important in themselves. Molly, however, enjoyed our walks immensely. If we encountered another dog, she would stop and greet it. If she saw something interesting, she would stop and explored fully. She spent most of our walks "smelling the roses" while I spent most of our walks imploring her to "come on, let's get going" on my dutiful march to my goal. She was living the moment; I was getting through it.[81]

He goes on to say that after having this realization, he

began to prioritize greeting people, enjoying the scenery and nature. Molly, wise Molly, had taught him to live in the moment.

I was reminded of the value of focusing on the moment while visiting the Church of Saint Lazarus in the West Bank Palestinian village of Bethany. The Church had a painting of Jesus with Mary and Martha. The painting is based on a story, from the Gospel of Luke about Jesus visiting his friends. During the visit, Mary is centering her attention on Jesus, and Martha is obviously annoyed because she is concerned about all the household tasks she has to do and

wants Mary to help her. The Latin inscription on the painting translates as, "'Martha, Martha,' the Lord said, 'You are worried and upset by many things.'" The complete quote from the Gospel continues thus: "... there is need of only one thing. Mary has chosen, the better part, which will not be taken from her." The dog in the painting also appears to have understood the Lord's message, as he is totally focused on Jesus.

BRING JOY AND BE OF SERVICE TO OTHERS

DOGS BRING JOY TO people – no matter what station they hold in life, or how famous, unknown, rich, or poor. Is there anything more joyful to behold than a child with his or her first puppy? It's not easy to determine who is happier – the pup or the child. One of the most moving stories I have ever read was about the momentary joy a dog can bring prisoners considered subhuman by their guards. The Jewish philosopher Emmanuel Levinas described this phenomenon in one of his essays about life in a prisoner of war camp:

> And then, about halfway through our long
> captivity, for a few short weeks, before the

sentinels chased him away, a wandering dog
entered our lives. One day he came to meet this
rabble as we returned under guard from work.
He survived in some wild patch in the region of
the camp. But we called him Bobby, an exotic
name, as one does with a cherished dog. He
would appear at morning assembly and was
waiting for us as we returned, jumping up and
down and barking in delight. For him, there
was no doubt that we were men.[82]

This story reminded me of how author Susanna Weiss
describes her dog encountering the homeless in a park:

My dog went to each man, and each smiled and
petted him. And then he kissed them. He reached
up to their faces and gave two or three little "kiss
licks." They bent to accept them and smiled some
more. My eyes filled with tears. Who kisses these
homeless men and women? They may receive
small gifts of charity from the few who don't pull
away in aversion and fear, but who kisses them?
My puppy dog, Dodger.[83]

Simply put, dogs make us happy, and when we come

home there is no doubt that we make them happy too. There are people we all know who could be described as always happy to see you. My dogs, when I come home, are always in that joyful, welcoming state. There is no other animal that demonstrates this genuine joy and excitement. What other animal has a rump extension whose main purpose is to let us know, 'I am so happy to see you?' At times it is so powerful that the tail seems to wag the dog. This joy can be contagious. As author Sarah Beasley writes of her dog in *Cosmo*, "He brought me so much joy, tenderness, and optimism, reminding me daily to tune in to my feelings and immediate needs, to prioritize smiling, laughing, and snuggling."[84]

In life, love and service go together. Dogs serve us in so many ways, but never grudgingly. It was relatively easy to

Sully, President H.W. Bush's service dog

enumerate those ways in Part IV. There is a reason some are called "service dogs." I was touched by Sully, President H.W. Bush's service dog in the photo of him lying at the casket of his master – a beautiful portrait of service and loyalty to the very end.

We have often heard the expression of gratitude, "thank you for your service" directed toward members of the military. Such an expression would also be most appropriate for the dogs who have served in the military and risked serious injury and even death in times of combat. There are countless examples of these heroic dogs and their invaluable service. They have been awarded medals and have been honored with permanent memorials.

A British Tommy and his dog during the First World War[85]

Yet even those dogs who are not officially designated "service dogs" manage to aid us in a myriad of ways. The truth is, we can all serve others in many ways – both big and small. Martin Luther King, in a speech which made reference to Jesus' exhortation, "The greatest among you will be your servant,"[86] concludes by outlining how all of us can be great:

> You don't have to have a college degree to serve.
> You don't have to make your subject and your verb
> agree to serve. You don't have to know about Plato
> and Aristotle to serve. You don't have to know
> Einstein's theory of relativity to serve. You don't
> have to know the second theory of thermo-
> dynamics in physics to serve. You only need a
> heart full of grace, a soul generated by love.
> And you can be that servant.[87]

Dogs don't have college degrees, nor do they know grammar or philosophy, but they *do* know how to love, serve, and bring joy to others. They set exceptional examples of these virtues throughout their whole lives and we are the ones who benefit from the examples they set. They are truly great.

BE FORGIVING

ADRIAN RAESIDE illustrates perfectly the capacity for forgiveness in dogs:

@raesidecartoon.com

Dogs don't hold grudges. They may pout for a while, but it never lasts. They are always ready to forgive and forget. They are always ready to begin anew. Of course, dogs want to be forgiven too. The research regarding whether dogs feel guilt or not is somewhat ambiguous.[88] Is it the tone in one's voice that results in *that* look, or them simply knowing that they did something wrong? Whatever the case, all dog owners notice when their dog looks guilty about something. Dogs can't fake innocence like humans can. All I have to say is, "What's this?" to my dogs after discovering a chewed shoe or a ripped up doggy bed in order to witness their obvious guilty reaction – the lowered head, the tail between the legs, that particular look in their eyes. Horowitz does not believe that dogs feel guilt, however, she explains, "Dogs have knowledge of a kind of category of *things one must never, ever do.*"[89] Humans can fake innocence and can also fake forgiveness. I am sure that most parents have experienced an insincere "SORRY!" when their children are told to apologize for something they did to a sibling. As parents, we often have to remind them that they actually should mean it when they say they are sorry. Dogs are not good fakers, and their forgiveness is always sincere. They never withhold their forgiveness, no matter what happens to them. It's not easy to follow their example, but they offer incredible lessons for cultivating forgiveness. Author Allan Lokos points out that despite not having been the kindest companion in the past, his dog always understood he was doing the best he could: "Beau did his best to teach me about forgiveness. He certainly was an example. During that difficult period of my life when I was such a poor companion to him, he shook off my faults and came back again and again with unbounded love."[90]

This is touchingly described in my friend Fiona's story about Nellie, the boxer she rescued. Nellie had been abused terribly in a puppy mill and was about to be euthanized. Despite the abuse she suffered, including lack of food and shelter, Nellie learned to trust again. This extraordinary capacity astounded Fiona enough to reflect upon it further:

How do these dogs forgive us? How do they enter into
their second chances with such indomitable spirit?
I marvel at their capacity to give love – and radiate
gratitude for whatever love comes their way. I am
humbled by every dog who has been a part of our
lives, whether it be for years or months. They ask
for so little and give so much. But most of all, I am
touched by their capacity to forgive and to trust again,
and again. I know that my life has been made richer
and fuller because of the dogs I have come to know
and love. I am gentler, more patient, less selfish,
and much kinder because that is what our dogs
have taught me.

Without a doubt, forgiveness heals, and lack of forgiveness leaves an open wound – sometimes one that lasts a
lifetime. A theologian once wrote that the only sin God cannot forgive is the sin of not wanting to be forgiven. Dogs
have important lessons to teach us in this regard. American Buddhist Lama Tsomo observed:

They forgive because they don't see the fun in
holding a grudge. They love again, even if their

hearts have been broken. If they make a mistake and we scold them, they don't justify or blame-push. They're simply crestfallen, telling us, "I'm sorry!" with their whole bodies until we smile at them again. Relationships can be so simple. Really.[91]

While perusing the internet looking for famous paintings with dogs, I came across Murillo's The Prodigal Son. In it, the son is welcomed by his forgiving father. This has always been my favorite parable. I frequently taught it to my university students and had them role play the different characters – the prodigal son who has disappeared and squandered his inheritance only to return home seeking forgiveness; the elder brother; the father; and the narrator (Jesus). I love the ending of the parable when the father says to the jealous elder brother, "But we had to celebrate and rejoice, because this brother of yours was dead and has come to life; he was lost and has been found."[92] Jesus teaches about seeking and being offered forgiveness, as well as rejoicing when a sinful person becomes grace-filled. The little dog in the painting appears to be as happy as the father in welcoming the prodigal son home. This parable is a concrete example of Jesus' exhortation to Peter who asked whether he should forgive someone as many as seven times. Jesus responds by saying, "Not seven times, but I tell you seventy-seven times."[93] This is a biblical number meaning an infinite number of times. Dogs seem to have an easier time with that number than us humans.

Bartolomé Esteban Murillo (1617-1682)

Be Loving and Loyal

In Homer's epic Greek poem *The Odyssey*, Odysseus returns home disguised as a beggar after an absence of twenty years. He is recognized, however, by Argos, a dog who lay sick and dying: "As they were thus talking, a dog that had been lying asleep raised his head and pricked up his ears. This was Argos, whom Ulysses had bred before setting out for Troy..."[94] Odysseus also recognizes Argos and sheds a tear at seeing him, but, "...Argos died as soon as he had seen his master."[95]

Dogs were not endowed with the complementary "man's best friend" label by being fair-weather friends. Although some will argue that dogs like us because we feed them and that they are really only scavengers, I do not accept this explanation. Why do we bond with other human beings? Are we really interested in an individual who does not care to be with us? Would our children still love us if we did not provide the necessities of life for them? Even when we do, there are times when teenagers would like all the advantages (like food and funds) of family life without bonding with anyone in the family. How different are dogs? Well, they are *more* loyal because even when they are mistreated and not provided for, they oftentimes still want to be with their masters. Writing about his dog Marley, John Grogan observed, "Mostly, he taught me about friendship and self-lessness and, above all else, unwavering loyalty."[96] Others feel the same way. Spiritual writer Mark Nepo has also acknowledged what his dogs have taught him: "I am more loving and more in the world because of their dogness, their unstoppable presence, and their unending love."[97] Scientist and Nobel Prize winner Konrad Lorentz wrote, "The bond with a true dog is as lasting as the ties of this earth will ever be."[98]

There are examples of those ties lasting beyond the grave. Take, for instance, a report from Italy about Tommy, a German shepherd who regularly waited for his mistress, Maria Lochi, when she attended church services in San Donaci. She had rescued Tommy and he accompanied her wherever she went. When she died, Tommy followed her casket into the church. Following the funeral, whenever the church bells rang, Tommy would show up at the church – presumably looking for his mistress. He would sit in front of the altar facing the congregation. He did not disturb the service and his presence was fondly accepted by all. Tommy died only a few months after the death of Mrs. Lochi, and it was believed that his death was precipitated at least in part by the death of his owner.[99]

This powerful bond is more than just a dog lover's wishful thinking. Neuroscientist Dr. Gregory Bearns at Tufts University researched dogs and observed that they want to be with us even when they don't need food or shelter. He concludes, "... if that wasn't love, then I would surely accept it as a reasonable facsimile."[100] Researcher John Bradshaw prefers to refer to a dog's love as "uncomplicated" instead of "unconditional." Whatever the adjective, the subject at hand is still love. Charles Darwin goes a step further, comparing a dog's devotion to a spiritual experience:

> The feeling of religious devotion is a highly
> complex one, consisting of love, complete
> submission to an exalted and mysterious superior,

a strong sense of dependence, fear, reverence, gratitude, hope for the future and perhaps other elements. No being could experience so complex an emotion until advanced in his intellectual and moral faculties to at least a moderately high level. Nevertheless we see some distinct approach to this state of mind, in the deep love of a dog for his master, associated with complete submission, some fear and perhaps other feelings.[101]

I do not see this view as entirely far-fetched. We provide for them, care for them, show affection and love for them, reward them, and punish them. In return they obey, provide love, affection, and loyalty. Roger A. Caras, the author of several books about dogs and other animals writes, "Dogs have given us their absolute all. We are the center of their universe. We are the focus of their love and faith and trust. They serve us in return for scraps. It is without a doubt the best deal man has ever made."[102] British veterinary surgeon and writer James Heriot would agree: "If having a soul means being able to feel love and loyalty and gratitude, then animals are better off than a lot of humans."[103] Philosopher and theologian Stephen H. Webb explored the unique relationship between the human, the dog, and the Divine:

"The interconnections among God, humans and dogs are rich. Both God and dogs love unconditionally, both God and humans are masters in their own realms, and both dogs and humans are creatures and servants. Humans are in between, both masters and servants, loved by God and dogs alike."[104] Interestingly, a poem commonly considered among the greatest in the English language, Francis Thompson's *The Hound of Heaven* compares God to a hound whose incessant hunt is meant to bring salvation to the sinner who flees God's salvific love: "I fled Him down the nights and down the days ..." One of the definitions of "to hound" someone is to "pursue relentlessly." God, the Hound, pursues us relentlessly, the lost sheep, who resist by fleeing into dead-end quests. Thompson, who experienced homelessness and addiction in his brief life, was a troubled soul, but nonetheless knew that despite his failures he was worthy of the love of the Hound of Heaven, who would never give up on him. In his comic *Bizarro*, Dan Piraro depicts a surprised soul arriving in heaven and seeing a dog as the Almighty seated on a throne.

We know that wolves, over time, evolved into dogs because of their interactions and relationships with humans. Humans helped this canine evolve into a trusted companion. But what about our evolution as human beings?

Have dogs helped us evolve into better creatures? There are those, like Jeffrey Moussaieff Masson, author of *The Dog Who Couldn't Stop Loving*, who believe, "Dogs made us humans in key ways. They helped to teach us, or the very least reinforced, how to love, to empathize, to trust, to play, (as adults, not only as children), to apologize – even in certain ways, how to communicate."[105] Lord Byron honored the enriching relationship he had with his beloved Newfoundland dog, Botswain, in his poem, *Epitaph To a Dog*, and had a monument built in memory of his faithful companion. Scholars believe that the introduction to the poem was written by Byron's friend John Hobhouse:

Near this spot
Are deposited the Remains
Of one
Who possessed Beauty
Without Vanity,
Strength without Insolence,
Courage without Ferocity,
And all the Virtues of Man
Without his Vices.

FINAL THOUGHTS

MY WIFE SUSAN AND I have developed what we call a "H.E.E." philosophy – a guide for making decisions that require a commitment and/or a financial investment. H.E.E. stands for Health, Ease, and Enrichment. In other words, if there is to be a particular commitment or purchase, it either has to be good for our health, make life's tasks easier, or be enriching spiritually, emotionally, culturally, etc. For example, we decided to buy an elliptical exercise machine. That expense, therefore, passed the health test. Regarding the ease test, I recently purchased a lawn tractor. I have quite a large property and the tractor certainly makes it easier to keep the property trim. As an example of the enrichment factor, Susan and I went on a pilgrimage to Israel and it truly was culturally and spiritually enriching. I am mentioning our commitment to the H.E.E. philosophy because I was thinking about how it would relate not only to our experience with our dogs, but also to the experiences of others with their dogs. Research has made it clear that dogs are good for our health. As previously mentioned, it has been shown that dog owners exercise more than individuals who do not own dogs. When I spend vacation time in Florida in the winter, I always see elderly people walking their dogs daily and I am certain these golden agers would not be exercising as much, if at all, if they didn't have a dog. I even witnessed an elderly lady in Florida walking her dog while using a walker! Dogs also lower our stress levels and help us to relax. So it's clear that dogs are good for our overall wellbeing.

It's also evident that dogs make some people's lives so much easier. Think of seeing-eye dogs whose masters would not be able to be as mobile without them, and those police dogs who help find lost people. Dogs make children feel more comfortable in court. They help find banned substances and keep us safe. They make it easier to detect certain types of cancer. Also, don't forget those saintly dogs who kept the pesky monkeys at bay and stood guard over the apple orchard. All in all, dogs definitely pass the enrichment test with flying colors. They teach us to live in the present, they bring joy to our lives, and teach us loyalty and service. Most importantly, they enrich our lives with uncomplicated love.

End Notes

[1] John Bradshaw, *The Animals Among Us: How Pets Make Us Human* (NY: Basic Books, 20017), Kindle Edition, 37.

[2] Yuval N. Harari, *Sapiens: a brief history of humankind* (N.Y: HarperCollins, 2014), 46.

[3] Adam Morey, 2006 (as cited in Adam Miklosi, 2015)

[4] Adam Miklosi, *Dog Behaviour, Evolution and Cognition,* (Oxford: Oxford Scholarship Online, 2015) 69.

[5] Bradshaw, 7.

[6] Ibid, 70.

[7] Jeffrey Moussaieff Masson, *Dogs never Lie About Love* (NY: Crown Publishers, 1997), 204.

[8] Meghan Murphy-Gill and Shanna Johnson, "Do Dogs Go To Heaven?" *US Catholic,* May, 20, 2016, www.uscatholic.org/articles/201605/do-dogs-go-heaven-30654.

[9] Ross D. Clark *Medical, Genetic and Behavioral Risk Factors of Siamese Cats* (Bloomington, IN: Xlibris) ebook.

[10] Stanley Coren, *The Intelligence of Dogs,* (NY: Bantam Books, 1994), 190.

[11] Alexandra Horowitz, *Inside of a Dog: What Dogs See, Smell and Know* (NY: Scribner, 2009) 62.

[12] Ibid.237.

[13] Eckhart Tolle, "Light Through Tapestry" in *The Dharma of Dogs: Our Best Friends as Spiritual Teachers,* ed. Tami Simon, (Boulder, Co: Sounds True, Kindle edition), 74.

[14] Miklosi, 81.

[15] Ibid, 87.

[16] Gladys Brown Edwards, *The New Complete Airedale Terrier* (London: Howell Book House, 1978), 24.

[17] Donna Long, *The best dogs in the World: Vintage Portraits of Children and Their Dogs,* (Berkeley: Ted Speed Press, 2007), 7.

[18] Raymond Coppinger and Mark Feinstein, *How Dogs Work,* (Chicago: Chicago University Press, 2015), 9.

[19] Jeffrey Moussaieff Mason, *The Dog Who Couldn't Stop Loving,* (NY: HarperCollins ebooks, 2010), Kindle edition, 240.

[20] Ibid, 668.

[21] Andrew Linzey, *Foreword to On Gods and Dogs: A Christian Theology of Compassion for Animals*, by Stephen H. Weber (NY: Oxford University Press, 1998), xi.

[22] Pope Francis, *Laudato Si: The encyclical letter on the care for our common home*, (2015).

[23] John Bosco, *Memoirs of the Oratory of Saint Francis de Sales*, trans. Daniel Lyons (New Rochelle, NY: Salesiana Publishers, 2012), Kindle edition, 97-99.

[24] Brother Ugolino, *The Little Flowers of St. Francis of Assisi*, trans. Roger Hudleston (Heritage Press, N.Y.) Kindle edition, 902.

[25] https://www.ewtn.com/library/MARY/flowers1.htm

[26] http://www.mycatholicsource.com/mcs/dusub/animals_in_church_history_saints_and_animals.htm

[27] https://catholic-animals.com/

[28] www.op.org/en/content/hounds-lord-little-known-meaning-dominican-dog

[29] http://www.newadvent.org/cathen/02503b.htm

[30] Margo A. Halm, "The Healing Power of the Human Animal Connection." *TheAmericanJournalofCriticalCare*,17no.4(July,2008):373,http://citeseerx.ist.psu.edu/viewdoc/download?doi=10.1.1.500.2269&rep=rep1&type=pdf

[31] Coren, 157-158

[32] Marguerite O'Haire, "Companion animals and human health: Benefits, challenges, and the road ahead" *Journal of Veterinary Behaviour*, no.5 (2010):226-234.

[33] 92.55(4) of the Florida Statutes

[34] http://companionsforcourage.org

[35] Tremblay, Isabelle, "Sundae donne du courage aux enfants." *Journal de Montreal* , Decembre, 7, 2018.

[36] Barker, and Kathryn S. Dawson, "The Effects of Animal -Assisted Therapy on Anxiety Ratings of Hospitalized Psychiatric Patients." *Psychiatric Services*, 49 no. 6 (1998):797. https://doi.org/10.1176/ps.49.6.797

[37] Julie Barton, How Losing My Dog Helped Me Believe There's an Afterlife" in *The Dharma of Dogs: Our Best Friends as Spiritual Teachers*, ed. Tami Simon, (Boulder, Co: Sounds True, Kindle edition), 193-194.

[38] Miklosi, 79.

[39] David Leonard Williams and Sarah Hogg, "The health and welfare of dogs belonging to homeless people." *Pet Behaviour* Science. 1 (2016): 23-30. https://pdfs.semanticscholar.org/52bf/f28cb0508a94aa1376597bceb1382b dof3ee.pdf

[40] Miklosi, 79.

[41] Bradshaw, 96.

[42] Jesse Feith, "The Dog that helps the homeless in Montreal." *Montreal Gazette*, January 6, 2018.

[43] Bradshaw, 96-97.

[44] "Pups and perps-what has four legs, a wet nose and helps young thugs grow up?" *The Economist* Dec.6, 2014.

[45] Wendy G. Turner, "The experiences of offenders in a prison canine program." *Federal Probation – A Journal of Correctional Philosophy and Practice* 71, no.1 (2007): https://www.uscourts.gov/statistics-reports/publications/federal-probation-journal

[46] Steve Widerman, "Sister is on a mission to help prisoners help others," *The Compass Official Newspaper of the Diocese of Green Bay*, March 14, 2013, https://www.thecompassnews.org.

[47] https://www.facebook.com/events/1384876795086307

[48] Halm, "The Healing Power," 373.

[49] Bradshaw, 210.

[50] Emily M. Sanford, Emma R. Burt and Julia E. Meyers-Manor, "Timmy's in the well: Empathy and prosocial helping in dogs," *Learning & Behavior* 46, no.4 (2018): 374-386 https://link.springer.com/article/10.3758%2Fs13420-018-0332-3

[51] Masson, *The Dog Who Couldn't Stop Loving*, 993.

[52] Miklosi, 89.

[53] Philippa Margaret Dall, Sarah Lesley Helen Ellis, Brain Martin Ellis, P. Margaret Grant, Alison Colye, Nancy Renee Gee, Malcolm Howard Granat, and Daniel Simon Mills.
"The influence of dog ownership on objective measures of free-living physical activity and sedentary behaviour in community-dwelling older adults: a longitudinal case-controlled study." *BMC public health* (June, 2017). https://link.springer.com/article/10.1186/s12889-017-4422-5#citeas

[54] Bradshaw, 292.

[55] Brittany Foster, "The Joy of Walking My Dog, Bernie" *Pulmonary Hypertension News*, August 7, 2020

56 "Montreal-Trudeau 75 years told" (Montreal: A Communications Chevalier publication, 2016)

57 Nicole Darrah, "Columbia drug gang reportedly put $70G hit on dog's Head," *Fox* News, July 26,2018, http://www.foxnews.com/world/2018/07/26/colombia-drug-gang-puts-70g-hit-on-dogs-head.html

58 David Grim, *Citizen Canine* (NY: Public Affairs, 2014), 224.

59 Bradshaw, 74.

60 Ibid. 77.

61 Ibid. 91.

62 Jean Houston, *Mystical Dogs* (Novato, California: New World Library, 2002), 36.

63 Carolyn G. Murphy, "Dix Choses Qu'on a apprises sur Max Domi a Tout le Monde en Parle," *Journal de Montréal*, 3 Fevrier, 2019.

64 https://www.journaldemontreal.com/2019/02/03/10-choses-que-lon-a-apprises-sur-max-domi-a-tout-le-monde-en-parle

65 Dawn A. Marcus, *Therapy Dogs in Cancer Care*, (NY: Springer,2012), 44

66 https://www.bedbugs.org/dogs/

67 Alexandra Horowitz, *Being a Dog: Following the Dog into a World of Smell*, (NY: Scribner, 2009), 20.

68 Masson, 240.

69 Stephen H. Webb, *On God and Dogs: A Christian Theology of Compassion for Animals* (NY: Oxford University Press, 1998), 98.

70 https://www.goodreads.com/author/quotes/4182.David_Steindl_Rast

71 QuotesRay, http://quotesray.com/author/saint-basil/quotes

72 Obituaries, *The Florida Catholic*, February 9-11, 2018

73 Masson, 83.

74 Bukkyo Dendo Kyokai, *The Teaching of Buddha*, (Honolulu: The Society for the Promotion of Buddhism, 2009) 90.

75 https://www.brainyquote.com/authors/abraham_maslow

76 Emily Dickson, "Forever is composed of Nows," Poetry Foundation https://www.poetryfoundation.org/poems/52202/forever-is-composed-of-nows-690

77 John Grogan, *Marley and Me*, (HarperCollins e-book, 2009) 279.

78 Dave Barry, *Lessons From Lucy, The Simple Joys of an Old, Happy Dog*, (New York, Simon and Schuster, 2019) 90.

[79] Houston, 56.

[80] Eckhart Tolle, *The Power of Now,* (Vancouver, B.C., Namaste publishing, 1999) 27.

[81] John Izzo, *The five secrets you must discover before you die,* (San Francisco, Berrett-Koehler, 2008) 88.

[82] Emmanuel Levinas, *Difficult Freedom Essays on Judaism,* trans. Sean Hand (Baltimore: Johns Hopkins University Press, 1990),153

[83] Susanna Weiss, "The Tail of My Perfect Teacher" " in *The Dharma of Dogs: Our Best Friends as Spiritual Teachers,* ed. Tami Simon, (Boulder, Co: Sounds True, Kindle edition), 92-93.

[84] Sara C. Beasley, "Cosmo Perry Wiggins – Fernandez Soucy-Beasley" in *The Dharma of Dogs: Our Best Friends as Spiritual Teachers,* ed. Tami Simon, (Boulder, Co: Sounds True, Kindle edition), 89.

[85] Imperial War Museum

[86] Mt 23:11 (NRSV).

[87] Martin Luther King, Jr., "The Drum Major Instinct" The Martin Luther King, Jr.Research and Education Institute Stanford University https://kinginstitute.stanford.edu/king-papers/documents/drum-major-instinct-sermon-delivered-ebenezer-baptist-church

[88] Adam Miklosi, "The Science of Friendship: Why dogs fit into families so well," *Scientific American* 27, no 4 (2018):20.

[89] Alexandra Horowitz, *Inside of a Dog: What Dogs See, Smell and Know,* (NY: Scribner, 2009), 228.

[90] Alan Loukas, "Golden Tails" in *The Dharma of Dogs: Our Best Friends as Spiritual Teachers,* ed. Tami Simon, (Boulder, Co: Sounds True, Kindle edition), 145.

[91] Lama Tsomo, "Lama Kusung" in *The Dharma of Dogs: Our Best Friends as Spiritual Teachers,* ed. Tami Simon, (Boulder, Co: Sounds True, Kindle edition), 34.

[92] Lk15:32 (NRSV).

[93] Mt18:21 (NRSV).

[94] Homer. *The Iliad and The Odyssey,* (Enhanced Media Kindle Edition), 553.

[95] Ibid, 553.

[96] Grogan, Marley, 280.

[97] Mark Nepo, "The Work of World" *The Dharma of Dogs: Our Best Friends as Spiritual Teachers,* ed. Tami Simon, (Boulder, Co: Sounds True, Kindle edition), 204.

98 "Konrad Lorenz Quotes." BrainyQuote.com. Xplore Inc, 2018. 23 May 2018. https://www.brainyquote.com/quotes/konrad_lorenz_391899

99 King, Carol. *Italy's Devoted Church-going dog Dies Of A Broken heart After losing Owner.* Italy magazine, 26 Jan.2013. https://www.italymagazine.com/italy/tommy/italy-s-devoted-church-going-dog-dies-broken-heart-after-losing-owner.

100 Gregory Bearns, *How dogs Love Us,* (Seattle: Lake Union Publishing, 2013, Kindle) 194.

101 Charles Darwin, and False, *The Principal Works of Charles Darwin: the Origin of Species. The Descent of Man.* (John B. Alden, Publisher, 1886) *Nineteenth Century Collections Online,* http://tinyurl.galegroup.com/tinyurl/ACtxu7, 52.

102 Roger A Caras, Goodreads, https://www.goodreads.com/quotes/37507-dogs-have-given-us-their-absolute-all-we-are-the

103 Stephen H. Webb, *On God and Dogs: A Christian Theology of Compassion for Animals* (NY: Oxford University Press, 1998) 179.

104 Ibid, 124.

105 Masson, *The Dog Who Couldn't Stop Loving,* 1095.

Bibliography

Barker, Sandra B. and Kathryn S. Dawson, "The Effects of Animal -Assisted Therapy on Anxiety Ratings of Hospitalized Psychiatric Patients." *Psychiatric Services*, 49 no. 6 (1998).

Barry Dave, *Lessons From Lucy, The Simple Joys of an Old, happy Dog*. New York: Simon and Schuster, 2019.

Bearns, Gregory, *How dogs Love Us*. Seattle: Lake Union Publishing, 2013, Kindle edition.

Bosco, John, *Memoirs of the Oratory of Saint Francis de Sales*. Translated by Daniel Lyons. New Rochelle, NY: Salesiana Publishers, 2012. Kindle edition.

Bradshaw, John. *The Animals Among Us: How Pets Make Us Human*. New York: Basic Books, 2017. Kindle edition.

Brother Ugolino, *The Little Flowers of St. Francis of Assisi*, trans. Roger Hudleston N.Y. Heritage Press, Kindle edition.

Camosy, Charles. *For Love of Animals: Christian Ethics Consistent Action*. Cincinnati, OH: Franciscan Media, 2013.

Caras, Roger, *Treasury of Great Dog Stories*. New York: Galahad Books, 1990.

Clark, Ross D., *Medical, Genetic and Behavioral Risk Factors of Siamese Cats*. Bloomington, IN: Xlibris ebook

Coppinger, Raymond and Mark Feinstein, *How Dogs Work*. Chicago: Chicago University Press, 2015.

Coren, Stanley. *The Intelligence of Dogs*. New York: Bantam Books, 1994.

Dall, Philippa, Margaret Ellis, Brian Martin, Grant, P. Margaret, Colyer, Alison, Gee, Nancy Renee, Granat, Malcolm Howard, and Mills, Daniel Simon.

"The influence of dog ownership on objective measures of free-living physical activity and sedentary behaviour in community-dwelling older adults: a longitudinal case-controlled study." *BMC public health* (June, 2017).

Darwin, Charles, and False. *The Principal Works of Charles Darwin: the Origin of Species. The Descent of Man*. John B. Alden, Publisher, 1886.

Dickson, Emily, "Forever is composed of Nows." Poetry Foundation. https://www.poetryfoundation.org/poems/52202/forever-is-composed-of-nows-690

Eames, Ed and Toni Eames, *Partners in Independence, A Success Story of Dogs and the Disabled.* New York: Howell book House, 1997.

Edwards, Gladys Brown, *The New Complete Airedale Terrier.* London: Howell Book House, 1978.

Eisenman, Andrew, *Alexandra Horowitz, Author of Inside of a Dog.* Kindle Singles Interview.

Emmanuel, Levinas, *Difficult Freedom Essays on Judaism,* Translated by Sean Hand. Baltimore: Johns Hopkins University Press, 1990.

Emmons, Robert A., *Gratitude Works.* San Francisco: Jossey-Bass, 2013.

Stein, Garth, *The Art of Racing in the Rain.* N.Y.: HarperCollins,2008.

Graham, Tanya, *Dog Wisdom.* Glen Waverly, Australia: Blue Angel Publishing, 2005.

Grim, David, *Citizen Canine.* New York: Public Affairs, 2014.

Grogan, John, *Marley and Me.* N.Y.: HarperCollins, 2009.

Homer, *The Iliad and The Odyssey.* Translated by Samuel Butler. Lulu.com. 2016, Kindle Edition.

Harari, Yuval N., *Sapiens: a brief history of humankind.* N.Y.: Harper Collins, 2014.

Horowitz, Alexandra, *Being a Dog.* New York: Scribner, 2016.

___. *Inside of a Dog: What Dogs See, Smell and Know.* NY: Scribner, 2009.

Houston, Jean, *Mystical Dogs.* Novato, California: New World Library, 2002.

Izzo, John, *The five secrets you must discover before you die.* San Francisco: Berrett-Koehler, 2008.

___. *The five thieves of happiness.* Oakland, Ca.: Berrett-Koehler, 2017.

Ensminger, John, *Service and Therapy Dogs in American Society: Science, Law, and the Evolution of Canine Caregivers.* Springfield, Ill.: Charles C Thomas, 2010.

Kalman, Maria, *Beloved Dog.* New York: Penguin Press, 2015.

King, Martin Luther, "The Drum Major Instinct." The Martin Luther King, Jr.Research and Education Institute, Stanford University. https://kinginstitute.stanford.edu/king-papers/documents/drum-major-instinct-sermon-delivered-ebenezer-baptist-church

Kyokai, Bukkyo Dendo, *The Teaching of Buddha*. Honolulu: The Society for the Promotion of Buddhism, 2009.

Linzey, Andrew, *Creatures of the Same God, explorations in animal theology,* New York: Lantern Books, 2007.

Long, Donna, *The best dogs in the World: Vintage Portraits of Children and Their Dogs*. Berkeley: Ted Speed Press, 2007.

Lorenz, Konrad. "Konrad Lorenz Quotes." BrainyQuote.com. https://www.brainyquote.com/quotes/konrad_lorenz_391899

Marcus, Dawn. *Therapy Dogs in Cancer Care*. NY: Springer, 2012.

Martin, James, *Becoming who you are*. Mahwah, N.J.: Hidden Spring, 2006.

Masson, Jeffrey Moussaieff. *Dogs never Lie About Love*. New York: Crown Publishers, 1997.

McCutcheon, Paul and Susan Weinstein. *The New Holistic Way for Dogs and Cats, The Stress-Health Connection*. Berkeley: Celestial Arts, 2010.

Miklosi, Adam, "The Science of Friendship: Why dogs fit into families so well," *Scientific American* 27, no 4 (2018):20.

———, Adam, *Dog Behaviour, Evolution and Cognition* Oxford: Oxford Scholarship Online, 2015.

Murphy-Gill, Meghan and Shanna Johnson, "Do Dogs Go To Heaven?" *US Catholic*, May, 20, 2016. www.uscatholic.org/articles/201605/do-dogs-go-heaven-30654.

O'Haire, Marguerite, "Companion animals and human health: Benefits, challenges, and the road ahead" *Journal of Veterinary Behaviour*, no.5 (2010).

Robitaille, Joel A., *A Dog's Religion*. Goodreads, 2011. Kindle edition.

Saunders, Marshall, *Beautiful Joe*. SMK Books, 2014. Kindle

Simon, Tami, ed. *The Dharma of Dogs: Our Best Friends as Spiritual Teachers*. Boulder, Co: Sounds True, 2017, Kindle edition.

Stein, Garth, *The Art of Racing In The Rain*. New York: Harper, 2009.

Thompson, Francis, *The Hound of Heaven*. New York: Dodd, Mead and
    Company, 1926.

Tolle, Eckhart, *The Power of Now*. Vancouver, B.C.: Namaste publishing, 1999.

Turner, Wendy G., "The experiences of offenders in a prison canine
    program." *Federal Probation – A Journal of Correctional Philosophy
    and Practice* 71, no.1 (2007). https://www.uscourts.gov/statistics-
    reports/publications/federal-probation-journal

Twain, Mark, *A Dog's Tale*. New York: Harper and Brothers, 1904.

Webb, Stephen H., *On God and Dogs: A Christian Theology of Compassion
    for Animals*. New York: Oxford University Press, 1998.

CPSIA information can be obtained
at www.ICGtesting.com
Printed in the USA
BVHW041747070421
604344BV00012B/1044